Psychopharmacology and Psychotherapy

Strategies for Maximizing Treatment Outcomes

Mental Health Practice Under Managed Care
A Brunner/Mazel Book Series

S. Richard Sauber, Ph.D., Series Editor

The Brunner/Mazel Mental Health Practice Under Managed Care Series addresses the major developments and changes resulting from the introduction of managed care. Volumes in the series will enable mental health professionals to provide effective therapy to their patients while conducting and maintaining a successful practice.

3. Solution-Oriented Brief Therapy of Adjustment Disorders: A Guide for Providers Under Managed Care
   By Daniel L. Araoz, Ed.D., and Marie A. Carrese, Ph.D.

2. Group Psychotherapy and Managed Mental Health Care: A Clinical Guide for Providers
   By Henry I. Spitz, M.D.

1. Psychopharmacology and Psychotherapy: Strategies for Maximizing Treatment Outcomes
   By Len Sperry, M.D., Ph.D.

Mental Health Practice Under Managed Care, Volume 1

Psychopharmacology and Psychotherapy

Strategies for Maximizing Treatment Outcomes

Len Sperry, M.D., Ph.D.

Brunner/Mazel *Publishers* • New York

Library of Congress Cataloging-in-Publication Data

Sperry, Len.
Psychopharmacology and psychotherapy : strategies for maximizing treatment outcomes / Len Sperry.
p. cm.– (Mental health practice under managed care ; 1)
Includes bibliographical references and indexes.
ISBN 0-87630-787-X
1. Mental illness–Treatment. 2. Managed mental health care.
3. Multimodal psychotherapy. I. Title. II. Series.
[DNLM: 1. Mental Disorders–therapy. 2. Mental Health Services–trends. 3. Managed Care Programs. 4. Psychopharmacology–trends.
5. Psychotherapy–trends. 6. Treatment Outcome. WM 400 5751p 1995]
RC480.5.S644 1995
616.89'1–dc20
DNLM/DLC
for Library of Congress 95-21881
CIP

Published by
BRUNNER/MAZEL, Inc.
19 Union Square West
New York, New York 10003

Manufactured in the United States of America

10 9 8 7 6 5 4 3 2 1

To Dr. Richard H. Cox, an esteemed teacher, clinician, and colleague.
It was in team-teaching of psychopharmacology with him that
I first became intrigued with the idea of combining
psychopharmacology and psychotherapy.

Acknowledgments

I would like to acknowledge the Series editor, Dr. Richard Sauber, and my editor at Brunner/Mazel, Natalie Gilman. A special thanks to Anna Kempf for her word processing efforts. I also commend my first mentors in managed care, Drs. Barry Blackwell and Kathy Schneider-Braus, who introduced me to the ins and outs of IPAs, PPOs, and the rest of the alphabet revolution while I was a fellow at the University of Wisconsin Medical School, Milwaukee Clinical Campus in 1984–1985. More recently, Dr. Harry Prosen, Chair of Psychiatry at the Medical College of Wisconsin has enriched my understanding of health service delivery and the changing roles of mental health clinicians.

I began my psychopharmacology training under the able tutelage of Dr. Ron Cromwell and am proud to have been his student. The ideas in this book have been "field tested" with several classes of psychiatry residents and clinical psychology graduate students. I thank them for their input and feedback. I'm also pleased that three Medical College of Wisconsin colleagues, Drs. Steve Moffic, Kathryn Krieg, and Harold Harsch, were able to contribute their expertise to the chapters in Part IV. Each is highly regarded for his or her ability to translate psychopharmacological and psychotherapeutic strategies with inpatients and older adults in managed care settings. I much value their contributions to this volume.

Contents

Foreword by Jan Fawcett, M.D. ix

Preface xi

PART I: MENTAL HEALTH AND MANAGED CARE

1. *Changing Roles in Mental Health Services* 3
2. *The Evaluator Role Function* 11
3. *The Provider Role Function* 20
4. *The Consultor Role Function* 23

PART II: GENERAL TREATMENT STRATEGIES AND GUIDELINES

5. *Combining Treatment Modalities* 35
6. *Ensuring Medication Compliance and Treatment Adherence* 49
7. *Incorporating Psychoeducational Strategies* 59
8. *Preventing Relapse and Recurrence* 68

PART III: SPECIFIC TREATMENT STRATEGIES AND GUIDELINES

9. *Anxiety Disorders* 79
10. *Bipolar Disorder* 95
11. *Depression* 105
12. *Schizophrenia* 113
13. *Personality Disorders* 124

PART IV: SPECIAL APPLICATIONS

14. *Inpatient Treatment*
by H. Steven Moffic, M.D., and Kathryn Krieg, M.D. 141

15. *The Older Adult*
by Harold Harsch, M.D. 156

References 173

Name Index 187

Subject Index 190

Foreword

This book is well worth reading because it is unique in addressing *process* in strategies for maximizing therapeutic outcomes in the treatment of psychiatric patients. This is true both with respect to the effective integration of psychotherapy and psychopharmacology, and in addressing changes in the context of the practice of psychiatry in the direction of managed care, as dictated by the changing economics of health care.

One major way that psychiatry is different from other medical disciplines is its emphasis on process as well as content. Attention to process is stressed along with the diagnostic interview, as well as in learning to interact therapeutically in psychotherapy. It is curious then, that advances in the content of our scientific knowledge, with the development of psychopharmacology over the past 30 years, have been, for the most part, considered in a vacuum regarding the process of effectively using psychopharmacology beyond the "cookbook" issues of drug choice, dosing regimens, algorithms, and augmentation strategies. The importance of individual patient characteristics, as well as the distinctive issues involved in the treatment of various conditions, are given relatively little attention as factors in the successful administration of psychotropic medications, perhaps because psychopharmacology was not embraced by psychiatrists practicing psychodynamic psychotherapies in its early days of development. Even today little is written on the integration of psychopharmacologic treatment, which casts the psychiatrist as a physician responsible for the treatment of a patient with an illness, and psychotherapy, which emphasizes the responsibility of the patient to learn from a therapist-teacher who guides the therapy. This is a process issue, crucial to obtaining good outcomes, that has been relatively ignored by both expert psychopharmacologists and dynamically oriented psychiatrists. Dr. Sperry addresses this omission from the available literature both in terms of issues relating to individual patient differences and differences relating to various disorders likely to benefit from combined treatment.

This book goes on to address the issues involved in determining what treatment goals and treatment combinations are appropriate to pursue in the present economic treatment context, which is based on the needs of the individual patient. Dr. Sperry goes beyond the "protest stage" to ask: What can the treating psychiatrist do that will be most helpful to a specific patient with a given disorder in the current presently existing treatment context? This is the issue that the contemporary psychiatrist must address in order to be of maximum value to patients. It is up to the present day psychiatrist to bring the maximum benefit of what has been learned to each patient. This book fundamentally addresses the question: How can we bring the best of what is available to our patients, given the reality of their health-care coverage? After all, our knowledge is only of value if we can maximally apply it for the benefit of our patients.

Jan Fawcett, M.D.
Stanley G. Harris, Sr. Professor and Chairman
Department of Psychiatry
Rush-Presbyterian-St. Luke's Medical Center

Preface

The 1990's may prove to be one of the most challenging eras that psychiatry and other mental health disciplines have faced. That there are powerful economic forces impacting clinical practice is a given. That there is confusion and demoralization among clinicians as the various mental health disciplines struggle to clarify their identity, role, and scope of practice is another given, albeit a painful one. But amidst the ferment and turmoil of all this change is an exhilarating challenge that most mental health professionals can and will be able to meet and master. Meeting and mastering the challenge will demand a number of modifications both in the conceptualization of psychiatric treatment and its delivery. Specifically, both the roles and the practice patterns of clinicians must change. It is this matter of roles and clinical practice patterns and strategies that is the focus of this book.

First, the book addresses the issues of roles. Part I describes the evolution of roles and identity among the various mental health disciplines, and describes the role functions of evaluator, provider, and consulter. For example, as mental health service delivery enters the 21st century, the special capacity for combined use of psychotherapy and psychopharmacology will distinguish prescribing clinicians, usually psychiatrists, from non-prescribing clinicians.

Second, the book addresses the matter of clinical practice patterns and treatment strategies. With the demand for outcome-oriented, time-limited, cost-effective treatment, it will no longer be sufficient for a clinician to provide a clinician-oriented treatment approach. Instead, treatment will be considerably more patient-oriented. In other words, the clinician will be expected to offer tailored treatment: determining which features of the illness, at what particular time in the course of illness, in which particular therapeutic setting, according to what treatment guideline, and, most importantly, taking into account the patient's expectation, explanatory model, and readiness for change. Accordingly, Part II of the book elaborates four overlapping therapeutic strategies that will assist the clinician in conceptualizing and providing such tailored, focused treatment. The four therapeutic strategies are: combine treatment modalities, enhance compliance and treatment adherence, incorporate psychoeducational interventions, and prevent relapse and recurrence.

Part III of the book applies these interconnecting therapeutic strategies to the most common psychiatric disorders seen in outpatient clinical practice. Separate chapters articulate specific treatment guidelines for the effective, integrative treatment of the anxiety disorders, bipolar disorder, depression, schizophrenia, and the personality disorders.

As noted, this book is primarily directed toward the treatment of adults in outpatient contexts. However, since the "worlds" of inpatient and outpatient practice continue to overlap, and because the effective treatment of older adults requires certain modifications in treatment planning and implementation, separate chapters with specific therapeutic strategies and treatment guidelines geared toward inpatient practice and the older adult comprise Part IV of the book.

There is much talk about the polarization in mental health today between the biological orientation and the psychotherapeutic orientation and between academic psychiatry and clinical practice. A recent study unexpectedly found that the supposed polarization between biological and psychotherapeutic, between academic and clinical, existed only in general attitudes that were surveyed. However, when psychiatrists were asked to respond clinically to specific case material, these polarized attitudes seemed to recede. Instead, the spectrum of clinicians studied showed remarkably similar thinking about specific treatment matters. The authors of this study concluded that the majority of clinicians practiced in integrated, combined types of treatment (Sullivan et al., 1993). In a recent editorial, Fawcett (1994) commented that psychiatry's challenge is to "combine the best of psychopharmacologi cal treatments with the best and most appropriate psychotherapeutic treatment tailored to both the disorder and the characteristics of the individual patient, while delivering it 'cost-effectively'" (p. 280). This is the challenge for psychiatry and the other mental health disciplines for this decade and the next. Hopefully, *Psychopharmacology and Psychotherapy: Strategies for Maximizing Treatment Outcomes* will provide mental health professionals some of the skills needed for meeting and mastering this challenge, as well as a vision for the future.

Part I

Mental Health and Managed Care

1

Changing Roles in Mental Health Services

I can vividly recall my first day of college in the early 1960's and seeing a poster celebrating the mental health care term in action. A male psychiatrist was in the forefront, with a nurse, social worker, psychologist, psychiatric aide, and chaplain in the background. The identity and role of the psychiatrist was clearly that of expert healer as well as leader of the treatment team composed of other disciplines in supportive roles. Now, however, the identity and role of the psychiatrist is not quite so clear, particularly in managed care settings. A rather common, stereotypic view of the managed care psychiatrist is of someone practicing second-rate medicine in a small back office, writing prescriptions, and signing off charts (Schneider-Braus, 1992). Today, a poster about managed care mental health might well show the psychiatrist in the background, serving in a supportive role and function!

That the identity and role of psychiatrists have changed considerably over the past 30 years is a given. How and why the psychiatrist's role has changed and the compatibility of this change with the values and ideals of psychiatry and the needs of managed care are the focus of this chapter. As background for discussing the evolving role of the psychiatrist, it will be useful to define terms and the context for these changes, including the evolving role of nonmedical therapists.

Professional identity refers to the image and self-concept attributed to members of a particular profession by those inside as well as outside that profession. Professional role refers to specific expectations regarding appropriate behavior for members of a given profession. Role function refers to the characteristic patterns or ways of fulfilling expectations. While identity defines what a professional is, role and role function prescribe what the professional does or should do.

Giles (1993) has captured the essence of the traditional role of psychiatrists in the following characterization: they were leaders in providing and administering mental health services, they prescribed and monitored medications and provided other medical services; they assumed primary responsibility for supervision of other therapists' work; and they provided policy input at both the local and national level. Today, Giles notes, psychiatrists not only command higher fees for outpatient services but–perhaps incorrectly–are perceived as willing to provide only longer-term, dynamically-oriented psychotherapy. Consequently, managed care firms refer patients instead to nonmedical therapists who practice shorter-term, goal-oriented therapies. And, when psychiatrists are retained, managed care administrators tend to limit the psychiatrist's role and influence. Giles also notes that because of their mistrust of psychiatrists, these administrators typically deny administrative positions to psychiatrists. Not surprisingly, this distrust and delimiting of role and influence have been demoralizing for many psychiatrists (Siegler, Axelband, & Isikoff, 1993).

Understandably, psychiatrists have mixed feelings about managed care, and generally have been less than enthusiastic in embracing managed care practice. Undoubtedly, many psychiatrists can recount numerous horror stories involving experiences with prior authorization, unreasonable demands for justification of continued care, denial of treatment, and premature discharge that have had various negative therapeutic consequences, including suicide (Westermeyer, 1991). Many are concerned about loss of autonomy in the way they choose to practice, loss of income, and the belief that managed care represents reduced quality of care. Unfortunately, organized psychiatry's response has been largely reactive and ambivalent. Since managed care has and will no doubt continue to shape the future of psychiatry, it is essential that psychiatrists become more proactive in articulating their unique identity and role. Failing this, psychiatry could further lose its leadership position–particularly its ability to influence policy–in the future of mental health delivery (Siegler, Axelband, & Isikoff, 1993).

THE CHANGING ROLE AND IDENTITY OF THE NONMEDICAL THERAPIST

Thirty years ago, the psychologist's function was primarily psychological assessment. Then, the social worker's function was taking a detailed social history and attending to the patient's social service needs. Similarly, the psychiatric nurse's function was administering medication and carrying out other medical orders. These role functions supported the psychiatrist's role as team leader and primary decision maker. Specific role functions of the psychiatrist included decisions about differential diagnosis and differential therapeutics, especially somatic therapies, like medication.

Outside the inpatient setting, this team concept has largely disappeared today. In place of differentiated roles that supported the psychiatrist as team leader, today social workers, psychologists, and psychiatric nurses are more likely to function in relatively autonomous capacities in diagnosing, deciding on, and providing psychosocial therapies in the role of "psychotherapists" or "nonmedical therapists."

In the past three decades, the identity of "psychotherapist" has evolved out of the unsuccessful efforts of psychiatry to retain "medical psychotherapy" as an exclusive role for those with the identity of licensed physicians (Ludwig, 1987). Now, "psychotherapist" is an inclusive identity and refers to social workers, psychologists, marital and family therapists, mental health counselors, pastoral counselors, and psychiatric nurses who practice various forms of psychotherapy or other psychosocial treatments. In the managed care literature, it is commonplace for the term "nonmedical therapist" to refer collectively to mental health professionals and to paraprofessionals who provide some form of psychotherapeutic service (Feldman & Fitzpatrick, 1992; Giles, 1993).

It should not be surprising that managed mental health care firms have a preference for short-term, goal-oriented therapies, and thus seek out providers who not only value but are skilled in providing this kind of treatment (Giles, 1993). Budman (1992) has described several value differences between those who champion short-term therapy compared to long-term therapy. For instance, long-term therapy emphasizes basic character change and sees participation in therapy as the patient's most important priority. Short-term therapy prefers the least radical intervention, does not endorse the concept of "cure," and views being in the world as more important than being in therapy. While long-term therapy posits that changes take place in the course of treatment, brief therapy accepts that many changes will occur "after therapy" because ultimately change occurs because of the patient's efforts and responsibility for implementing change.

Formal training and the attainment of certification or licensure mark the evolution of the identity and role of the nonmedical therapist in managed care practice. Whether their discipline is social work, psychologists, mental health counseling, or chemical dependency, these individuals have forged an identity and role that managed care administrators understand and appreciate as compatible with managed care policy. Presently, the same cannot be said for the identity and role of psychiatry. Of course, admitting inpatients and prescribing and managing medication are still largely the province of the psychiatrist, but whether and how long this continues is uncertain. Efforts to gain or increase prescription privileges have long been exerted by nonmedical therapists. In the meantime, others like Kisch (1991) and Sovner (1991) advocate an expanded role for nonmedical therapists in what they call "collaborative psychopharmacology," in which nonmedical therapists have increased input in decisions about medication and somatic treatments. Throughout this book, the more generic terms, "prescribing clinician" and "medical therapist," are used to refer to those individuals, such as psychiatrists, primary care physicians, nurse practitioners, physician assistants, and others who, by virtue of prescription privileges, can provide some or all of the role functions currently associated with the practice of psychiatry.

PROPOSED ROLE AND ROLE FUNCTIONS FOR PSYCHIATRISTS

Relatively little has been written about the developing identity and proposed alternative roles for psychiatrists. This section summarizes that literature. It also proposes and articulates an integrative role and role functions for psychiatrists or other prescribing clinicians in managed care.

The psychiatric community recognizes that changes in identity and role are necessary. Sabin and Borus (1992) contrast traditional fee-for-service psychiatric practice with managed care psychiatric practice with regard to role. They indicate that there is a major change in role involved: from independent professional in traditional practice to independent professional *and* employee partner in managed care practice. This implies a shift in role from an "authoritative" to a "collaborative" relationship with other mental health personnel. Others (Blackwell & Schmidt, 1992; McNutt, Severson, & Schomer, 1987) also advocate the collaborative role for the psychiatrist. To effect this role change, Blackwell and Schmidt (1992) conclude that psychiatrists need to be educated in four content areas: short-term therapy skills, ethical concerns, cost-efficient care, and professional role development. They believe that professional role development is learned through appropriate role modeling and supervised experiences in collaborative relationships with multiple providers from other disciplines. Sabin (1991) and Sabin and Borus (1992) suggest that six new skills are requisites of this role change: collaborative program development, individual practice management, ethical analysis, advocacy beneficence, developmental model, and a broad repertoire of treatment methodologies. Sabshin (1987) describes the changed role of the psychiatrist in the 1990's as that of a generalist who can integrate a mixture of combined techniques and will be able to titrate each, or move from one to the other with a diverse patient population.

These characterizations–collaboration, advocacy, short-term therapy, and integrative and combined interventions–stand in stark contrast to both the traditional image of the psychiatrist as an expert, authoritative team leader and the current stereotype of the managed care psychiatrist as a passive, prescription-writing functionary.

An evolution of the psychiatrist's role and role functions is underway, which will have a profound implication not only for managed care but also for psychiatric practice outside the managed care setting. This chapter proposes a specific integrative, collaborative role and three role functions for psychiatrists in managed care. The role is *maximizing psychotherapeutic and psychopharmacological outcomes.* The role functions are: *evaluator*, *provider*, and *consultor.*

Let us start by defining and articulating this role. Beginning with the word "outcomes," the managed care psychiatrist would conceptualize all treatment endeavors–from diagnosis to monitoring results of interventions–in terms of outcomes. This contrasts with traditional psychiatry's focus on process. Being outcome-oriented means concern about quality, efficacy, cost-effectiveness, and accountability.

The managed care psychiatrist's focus on outcome involves both psychotherapeutic and psychopharmacological interventions. I agree with Hyland (1991) that since medication has demonstrated effectiveness for a number of psychiatric conditions the question of psychopharmacology needs to be addressed in each patient evaluation. Similarly, the question of psychotherapy needs to be considered at the onset of every psychiatric treatment. Combined treatment, particularly integrating pharmacotherapy with psychotherapy, is the cutting edge of mental health today (Beitman, 1993a; Beitman & Klerman, 1991) and reflects psychiatry's biopsychosocial perspective.

Psychiatrists continue to maintain their primary role in psychopharmacology. However, there is considerable discussion about the involvement of psychiatrists in psychotherapy. Should they be primary providers of psychotherapy? Or be psychotherapy supervisors? Or, principal decision makers about psychotherapeutic management?

Ludwig (1987) reviews the psychiatrist's role in the practice of psychiatry from the mid-1800's through the present. He notes that psychiatry has played a dominant role in psychotherapy until recently when nonmedical therapists have challenged that role. Medical psychotherapy has been defined as "a series of medical procedures carried out by a physician trained to treat mental, emotional, and psychosomatic illness through relationships with the patient in an individual, group or family setting, utilizing verbal or nonverbal communication with the patient" (Katz, 1986). Ludwig (1987) believes that there is a difference between psychiatrists and nonmedical therapists when it comes to conceptualizing, approaching, and managing clinical problems with psychotherapeutic methods. He contends that psychiatrists are trained to conceptualize problems from a medical and biopsychosocial perspective and tend to think in terms of diagnosis, differential diagnosis, differential therapeutics, and prognosis more so than do nonmedical therapists. Regarding their approach and management of clinical problems, Ludwig says that "inculcated with a sense of medical responsibility and Aesculapian authority, psychiatrists have been trained to take authoritative stands when necessary and make life-and-death decisions, intervening when the potential of suicide or violence exists and resorting to hospitalization or restraint under certain circumstances" (Ludwig, 1987, p. 365).

In short, he believes that their medical training and experience enable psychiatrists to conduct psychotherapy in its broadest sense, since they can administer a wider variety of medical and psychosocial interventions than nonpsychiatrists. Munoz (1994) would agree, but extends the psychiatrist's role beyond provider and supervisor of psychotherapy. Munoz insists that the psychiatrist should be the principal strategist in psychotherapeutic management and should decide on matters of differential psychotherapeutics (Frances, Clarkin, & Perry, 1984). Presumably, this would include deciding on the setting, duration, focus, and specific interventions to be utilized by the assigned therapist.

As for the word "maximize," it is my contention that psychiatrists are the most qualified among the mental health disciplines to exercise leadership and accountability for insuring that quality mental treatment is provided that is both efficacious and cost effective. According to Jaques and Clement (1991), "in order to discharge accountability, a person in a role must have appropriate authority" (p. 8). Medical license and board eligibility or certification in psychiatry provides such authority. Speaking about managerial role, Jaques and Clement (1991) note that "every manager must be held accountable for the work of subordinates, but also for adding value to their work..., second, he or she must be held accountable for sustaining a team of subordinates who are capable of doing their work; and third, he or she must set direction for subordinates and get them willing to work alone, with him or her in that duration, that is to say, he or she must carry leadership accountability" (p. 111). It is my belief that psychiatrists can and should likewise carry leadership accountability by insuring that treatment outcomes are maximized.

Unlike the leadership style of the traditional psychiatrist, which tended to be authoritative–or even authoritarian, the leadership style of the managed care psychiatrist would be consultative and collaborative. Such a leader seeks input on decisions and expects others to be accountable for their work tasks, but ultimately makes and takes responsibility for certain treatment decisions and outcomes. And given current malpractice and liability statutes (Woodward, Duckworth, & Guthiel, 1993), the psychiatrist would necessarily have an oversight function.

In short, I propose that the psychiatrist or prescribing clinician in managed care settings be accountable for maximizing psychotherapeutic and psychopharmacological outcomes. Essentially, this means insuring that quality, cost-effective, and efficacious care are delivered. This does not mean that the psychiatrist provides all services, but rather that the psychiatrist has sufficient involvement and decisional authority for treatment offered by all providers involved with a given patient. And, because the psychiatrist is legally accountable for treatment outcomes, he or she must exercise an oversight function. Specifically, this means that all mental health personnel will be held accountable for their particular role functions. For instance, each provider would be accountable for maximizing his or her particular treatment outcomes, the case manager would be accountable for maximizing the coordination of various providers, and the managed care administrator would be accountable for maximizing cost effectiveness. In short, the psychiatrist's accountability would be to insure that all psychosocial and somatic treatment outcomes were maximized.

Supporting this proposed role change are three interrelated role functions: evaluator, provider and consultor. These role functions simultaneously promote collaboration with patients (evaluator and provider) and with other managed care personnel (consultor), reflect the realities of managed care policies, and respect and enhance the psychiatrist's medical training and the unique biopsychosocial perspective of psychiatry. Table 1 summarizes this change and evolution of role and role functions.

TABLE 1
Change and Evolution of the Scope of Roles for Mental Health Professionals

Time Frame / *Professional*	*Yesterday*	*Typical Managed Care Setting*	*Proposed*
psychiatrists/ medical therapists/ prescribing clinicians	differentiated and wide	delimited and differentiated	focused (evaluator, provider, consultor)
	authoritative/ leadership	subordinate/ supportive	collaborative leadership
nonmedical therapists	differentiated and narrow (social worker, nurse, psychologists, etc.)	undifferentiated and broad (nonmedical therapists)	focused
	subordinate/ supportive	independent (quasi)	interdependent/ collaborative

2

The Evaluator Role Function

Bennett (1993) describes contemporary managed care as atheoretical and highly pragmatic. He believes that the essence of managed care can be reduced to three questions: What does the patient need? How can the need be met? And, how do we know when this outcome is achieved? It is my conviction that these three questions essentially reflect the psychiatrist's evaluator role function. Answering these three questions goes beyond the traditional discipline (psychology, social work, nursing, psychiatry) boundaries and is based on demonstrated efficacy rather than on ideology.

In a number of respects, the evaluator role function described here is distinct from the traditional psychiatric evaluation. Traditionally, a psychiatrist performs a psychiatric evaluation consisting of a description of the present illness, past psychiatric history, a social and developmental history, and a mental status exam, all of which leads to a diagnostic formulation–usually in DSM-IV categories–and a treatment plan. While such an evaluation addresses to some extent the first and second questions, it seldom addresses the third managed care question. This is because the standard psychiatric evaluation process is largely a symptom narrative and insufficiently focused on the patient's level of functioning, coping resources, readiness, and capacity for treatment. Furthermore, while a diagnostic formulation summarizes the patient's symptomatic presentation with a diagnostic label (question 1) and while the treatment plan may focus on symptomatic relief, it may not reflect how the patient's need can be best met (question 2). And, of course, the traditional psychiatric evaluation was not designed to address issues of accountability nor the monitoring of outcomes (question 3).

The proposed evaluator role function is, then, both broader and more focused than the traditional diagnostic-oriented evaluation process and role. While the traditional evaluation emphasizes data and content, the treatment-oriented evaluation emphasizes function and prognosis or treatability, that is, the extent to which a patient expects, is willing, and is able to modify or change behavior, as well as the patient's level of functioning, deficits, and coping resources. The evaluator engages in focused listening, that is, listening to the patient's story and symptom narrative for prognostic indicators and for clues regarding potential therapeutic leverage. Therapeutic leverage refers to the change potential that accrues from prognostic factors and treatment interventions that unbalance the patient's dysfunctional pattern of functioning and perpetuants, thereby increasing treatability and therapeutic outcomes.

Such an evaluation would consist of seven dimensions–seven P's: presentation, predisposition, precipitant, pattern, perpetuant, prognosis, and (treatment) plan (Sperry, Gudeman, Blackwell, & Faulkner, 1992). Of these, the dimensions of pattern, prognosis, and plan are most critical and are central to all the psychiatrist's three role functions (see Figure 1).

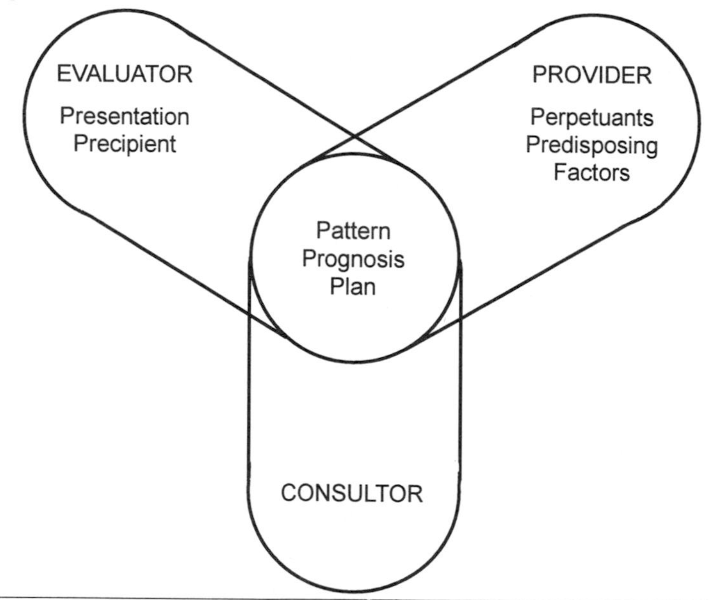

Figure 1. The Interrelationship of the Evaluator, Provider, and Consultor Roles and the Centrality of Pattern, Prognosis, and Plan

Presentation refers to the patient's symptoms, mental status, diagnosis, and perception of need. *Pattern* refers to the patient's consistent and predictable behavioral and emotional response and functioning in the face of specific triggers and stressors. *Perpetuants* refer to intrapersonal, interpersonal, and environmental factors that serve to reinforce and confirm the patient's pattern of functioning. *Prognosis* refers to the patient's treatability and expected response to treatment.

While arriving at a DSM-IV Axis I and II diagnosis may be necessary for record-keeping purposes, diagnosis has limited value in planning or implementing treatment (Beutler & Clarkin, 1990). On the other hand, knowledge of a patient's pattern can be of inestimable value in treatment planning and implementation. Pattern consists of predictable triggers and responses, as well as an explanation for the patterned response. While triggers and responses are observable phenomena, the explanation must be inferred, and, as in any clinical formulation, this inference can range from psychoanalytic, cognitive, or biological to a biopsychosocial explanation.

For instance, a shy, inhibited individual may exhibit a pattern of responding with avoidance and anxiety to triggers like close interpersonal relationships or public appearances. The explanation may be that the individual avoids because she anticipates that others will be critical and disapproving, and she sees herself as inadequate and socially awkward. Similarly, the perfectionistic individual may react to deadlines (trigger) with procrastination and excuse making (response) because he fears that making a mistake or wrong decision will prove his worthlessness (explanation).

Knowledge of patterns can facilitate establishing a treatment plan and strategies and tactics for accomplishing it. For example, a 23-year-old single male who is beginning therapy describes quitting jobs and leaving intimate relationships (responses) when the job demands more than minimal performance or the relationships require an increasing level of commitment (triggers). Further inquiry suggests that he perceives such demands as unreasonable and that if he cannot have things his way, he exits the situation (explanation). Therapy could focus on triggers, responses, or explanation, or on all of these. With regard to triggers, it could be suggested that he seek out jobs or relationships that place lesser demands on him, or that he be assisted to better cope with existing expectations and demands, or even reframe the demands. This represents a problem-focused or solution-focused treatment strategy.

Similarly, the patient could be helped to develop more adaptive responses. He could reverse some of his social skills deficits such as negotiation of job performance, increased stress tolerance, and assertiveness. Neither of these two treatment foci require genetic or transference interpretations or cognitive restructuring. However, treatment could also focus on the explanatory component, and cognitive restructuring and interpretation might be utilized. In short, pattern analysis is essential to evaluation and treatment planning in treatment settings where time is of the essence.

Completing a treatment-focused evaluation requires somewhat different information from the patient and corroborators since the emphasis is on prognosis and treatability.

Treatability is a function of both readiness and level of functioning. I have found it useful to think about readiness as involving three components: treatment expectations, treatment willingness, and treatment capability.

Regarding *treatment expectations*, research confirms the clinical observation that patients with moderate to high expectations of improvement do in fact respond better than those patients with minimal or no expectation of improvement (Sotsky et al., 1991). For this reason, I find it useful to elicit the patient's degree of expectation for improvement and then establish how realistic that expectation is. I then rate it on a 10-point scale with 1 being "very unrealistic" and 10 being "very realistic" (see Figure 2).

Treatment willingness is a term to designate the patient's change potential. This potential for change can be assessed in terms of a set of normative stages of change designated as: precontemplation, contemplation, action, or maintenance (Prochaska & DiClemente, 1986).

Precontemplation is the stage in which individuals do not intend to make changes in their lives or behavior. They either are unaware or only minimally aware of their problems, although others around them are quite aware and usually quite concerned. If they appear for treatment in this stage, they will deny they have a problem or need therapy. Thus, they tend to experience treatment as coercive and will respond with various forms of resistance, depending on their personality style. That is, they may reject a diagnostic label or medication trial outright, or they may passively accept a prescription yet be noncompliant. At this stage, even the involvement of the patient's family or legal coercion may fail to reverse noncompliance or nonadherence.

FUNCTIONAL PSYCHIATRIC EVALUATION SHEET

*Patient's Name:*__________________ *Age:* ___ *Intake Date:* ______

TREATMENT HISTORY: ________________________________

PRESENTATION: ________________________________

PATTERN: ________________________________

PRECIPITATING FACTOR(S): ________________________________

PREDISPOSING FACTOR(S): ________________________________

PERPETUATING FACTOR(S): ________________________________

PROGNOSTIC FACTOR(S):
Treatability (Exp + W + C3P) + Functioning

Tx Expectations	Tx Willingness	Tx Capability	Functioning Level				
10 Very Realistic	10	10	10	10	10	10	10
9	9 Maintenance	9 Psychotherapy	9	9	9	9	9
8	8	8	8	8	8	8	8
7	7 Action	7 Skill Deficit	7	7	7	7	7
6	6	6	6	6	6	6	6
5	5 Decision	5 Escape Behavior	5	5	5	5	5
4	4	4	4	4	4	4	4
3	3 Contemplation	3 Tx Sabotage	3	3	3	3	3
2	2	2	2	2	2	2	2
1 Very Unrealistic	1 Precontemplate	1 Parasuicidal	1	1	1	1	1
			Pi/Soc/Dgr/Occ/Sab				

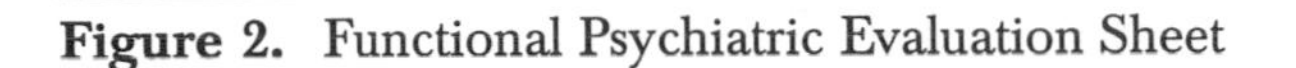

Figure 2. Functional Psychiatric Evaluation Sheet

Contemplation is the stage in which individuals are aware of their problem and will consider doing something about it, but have not yet made a commitment to action. Many psychiatric patients remain in this stage for long periods of time. They may accept a diagnosis but remain noncompliant or fail to adhere to a treatment regimen.

Action is the stage of change in which individuals assume responsibility for modifying themselves or their environment to overcome their problem. At this stage, compliance and adherence are least likely to be treatment issues.

Maintenance is the stage at which individuals work to consolidate treatment gains and prevent relapse. This stage may last a considerable period of time, usually beyond termination of regularly scheduled treatment sessions. Often, particularly with substance or behavioral addictions, maintenance may last a lifetime. Again, compliance and adherence are typically less problematic than at the precontemplation and contemplation stages.

Why is some measure or degree of Treatment Willingness/Stage of Change important? Patients who have accepted their diagnosis, decided to cooperate with treatment, and have made efforts to change are more likely to have positive treatment outcomes than patients who have not (Beitman, 1993b).

Stage of change can be assessed through interview, observation, or the 30-item Stage of Change Scale normed on a group of psychotherapy patients (McConnaughy et al., 1989). I have found it useful to rate Treatment Willingness/Stage of Change on a 10-point scale, with 1 representing Precontemplation, 3 Contemplation, 5 Decision for Action, 7 Action, and 9–10 Maintenance (see Figure 2).

Treatment Capability reflects the degree to which patients are capable of modulating or controlling their affects, cognitions, and behavior, and are thus psychologically available to collaborate in treatment. This contrasts with the psychological unavailability of patients who are continually parasuicidal or engage in treatment sabotage or escape behavior. Linehan (1987) describes five hierarchically arranged treatment targets: (1) parasuicidal behavior; (2) behaviors interfering with the conduct of therapy, such as missing or being late for sessions, noncompliance with medication, demanding behavior, inability or refusal to collaborate in treatment; (3) escape behaviors that interfere with a reasonable quality of life, such as substance abuse and antisocial or illegal behaviors; (4) social skills acquisition such as emotional regulation, modulation of behavior and impulses, self-management, and interpersonal effectiveness; and (5) achievement of the patient's personal goals.

Although these target goals were developed for borderline personality disordered patients, they have wider applicability. Obviously, patients who are parasuicidal or miss appointments are less capable of profiting from interpretation and insight than those who have sufficient social skills and the capacity to modulate and control affects and impulses. I have modified Linehan's hierarchical treatment targets and delineated them on a 10-point scale. On the Treatment Capability Scale, 1 represents parasuicidality, 3 treatment sabotage behavior, 5 escape behavior, 7 availability for work on skill acquisition, 9–10 availability for engaging in reconstructive psychotherapy (see Figure 2).

Overall level of functioning can be estimated by the Global Assessment of Functioning (GAF) Scale and the Global Assessment of Relationship (GARF) Scale of Axis V of DSM-IV. More specificity can be gained by including estimate of occupational functioning, social functioning, dangerousness, and substance abuse, in addition to the degree of psychological impairment, which is the overall measure of GAF. Kennedy (1992) specifies 10-point criteria for five subscales that I find particularly useful with rating patient functioning. Figure 3 shows my modification of Kennedy's subscales: "PI" represents psychological impairment, "Soc" represents social skills, "Dgr" represents dangerousness, "Occ" represents ADL-Occupational Skills, and "Sub" represents Substance Abuse.

To quickly and accurately gather such focused information requires considerable cooperation and collaboration by the patient and corroborators. Thus, efforts to establish rapport and engage the patient in the evaluation process are important for the psychiatrist functioning in the evaluator role as in the provider role. The following case illustrates this type of evaluation.

THE CASE OF C. W.

C. W. is a moderately obese, 38-year-old, never married, white, female clerk-stenographer who presented with a two-week onset of spontaneous crying, sad mood, decreased sleep with early morning awakening, and increasing social isolation. She had not shown up for work for four days, prompting the psychiatric referral. Her history and mental status exam are consistent with a diagnosis of major depressive episode, as well as meeting the criteria for avoidant personality disorder (*Presentation*). Cutbacks at her office had led to her being transferred out of a close-knit typing pool, where she had been for 16 years, to a receptionist-typist position for a new sales manager in another location. This transfer was viewed by her as a significant loss and appears to have triggered her depressive symptoms and social isolation (*Precipitant*).

No personal or family psychiatric or alcohol and substance abuse history was reported. However, C. W. described intense feelings of humiliation and rejection following the birth of a younger brother, after early nurturance by her parents. She came to believe that the opinions of others were all that counted. Yet, she was teased and ridiculed by her peers for her personal appearance, especially her obesity. There were also strong parental injunctions against discussing important matters with "outsiders" (*Predisposition*).

She typically distances and isolates herself from others, when she is in unfamiliar or in close interpersonal relations. Presumably, she anticipates and fears the disapproval and criticism of others. She views others as critical and harsh and is convinced she is viewed by others as inadequate. Therefore, she is slow to warm up to and trust others, and "test" others' trustability by being late for or cancelling or missing agreed-upon engagements (*Pattern*). Lack of social skills in relating to new or less-known individuals, and a limited social network–she is a "homebody" who spends much of her time reading romance novels, watching soap operas, or knitting–further contributes to an isolative lifestyle and reinforces her beliefs about self, the world, and others (*Perpetuants*).

With the exception of social relations she has functioned above average in all life tasks. She agrees she is severely depressed and wants to cooperate with combined treatment involving medication started and monitored on an outpatient basis along with time-limited psychotherapy. She does not appear to be particularly psychologically minded and has moderate skill deficits in assertive communication and in trust and friendship skills. It can be anticipated that she will have difficulty discussing personal matters with health providers and that she'll "test" and provoke providers into criticizing her for changing or cancelling appointments at the last minute, being late, and the like.

Nevertheless, she continues to be nicotine abstinent some three and half years after completing a smoking cessation program. Her support system includes some contact with an older female cousin and a pet dog. (*Prognosis*) Combined treatment with an antidepressant and psychotherapy focused on ameliorating symptoms, returning to work and establishing a supportive social network there; and increasing interpersonal skills were the initial treatment outcome goals established (*Plan*).

3

The Provider Role Function

The evaluator role function, then, emphasizes conceptualization and planning intervention based on treatability and patient functional capacity. The provider role function, on the other hand, emphasizes tailoring and combining treatment based largely on pattern, perpetuants, and prognosis.

Currently, medication management is the main provider role function for psychiatrists in outpatient managed care settings. Typically, the psychiatrist evaluates the appropriateness of medication for a patient referred from a nonmedical therapist. And if a medication trial begins, the psychiatrist monitors the individual weekly or biweekly until a maintenance dose is achieved. Thereafter, medication checks are scheduled monthly, bi-monthly and quarterly. These brief sessions, usually 15 or 20 minutes, provide an extraordinary opportunity to maximize treatment outcomes. Unfortunately, many psychiatrists skilled in managing the psychological issues of psychotherapy do not routinely utilize these skills when they provide medical treatment. Ward (1991) notes: "Too often, they neglect invaluable psychotherapeutic approaches and use only explanation and admonishment to get patients to take medication" (p. 69). It is not only possible, but highly probable that patients can achieve maximal pharmacological benefits within the context of an optimal patient-psychiatrist relationship.

Skilled medication management (Eckman, Liberman, Phipps, & Blair, 1990) requires awareness of the patient's pattern, prognostic factors, and overall treatment plan, particularly if the patient is concurrently involved in psychotherapy with a nonmedical therapist. An understanding of the psychology of medication compliance or adherence (Blackwell, 1976; Docherty, 1988) and the placebo effect (Beitman,

1993b; Spiro, 1986) is likewise important. Involvement of family members in insuring medication compliance (Docherty, 1988; Doherty & Baird, 1983) is also crucial.

The psychiatrist must consider what type of relationship–that is, how much dependency to allow the patient and how much authority to exert with the patient–he or she will strive to develop. In addition, the psychiatrist must negotiate a treatment agreement that maximizes medication compliance and placebo effect, as well as considering psychological reactions to dosage, side effects, main effects, and the influence of the patient's social network on compliance. Furthermore, transference reaction must be anticipated and recognized as it may either facilitate or sabotage treatment outcomes, as well as countertransference reactions that may distort proper management (Busch & Gould, 1993).

Ward (1991) describes specific strategies for effectively dealing with narcissistic, obsessive, histrionic, borderline, avoidant, schizophrenic, and paranoid patients in medication management contexts. Ward also provides a number of useful guidelines for structuring and tailoring management sessions based on the patient's treatment expectations and other prognostic factors.

The other psychiatric provider role function involves combined treatment, which has been heralded as the basis of clinical psychiatry practice in the twenty-first century (Beitman, 1993a). In this context, the psychiatrist sees the patient and provides combined treatment: medication and psychotherapy. The sessions may be scheduled for 30, 45, or 50 minutes, depending on the managed care policy and the psychiatrist's training and experience. The nature of the psychotherapy may be supportive, interpersonal, cognitive, dynamic, or strategic in focus. In addition to utilizing the same kind of strategies noted above for medication management, the psychiatrist works to maximize psychotherapeutic outcomes.

Most psychiatrists are familiar with the early results of the NIMH Treatment of Depression Collaboration Research Project (Elkin et al., 1989) wherein cognitive therapy or interpersonal therapy was combined with antidepressant treatment. However, fewer psychiatrists are aware of numerous other efforts to combine psychosocial modalities with medications for specific Axis I and Axis II disorders.

Beitman and Klerman (1991) offer cogent guideline and protocols for combining and tailoring medication and psychotherapy for various psychiatric disorders. There are other forms of combined treatment, such as medication and family therapy, medication and group therapy, and individual with family and marital therapy (Beitman, 1993a; Glick, Clarkin, & Goldsmith, 1993). These and other combined biopsychosocial interventions will further enhance the psychiatrist's efforts in maximizing psychopharmacology and psychotherapy. Parts II and III of this book detail strategies and guidelines for combining treatment and maximizing treatment outcomes.

THE CASE OF C. W. (Continued)

The treatment plan for C. W. was developed based on her presentation as well as on her pattern and prognostic factors. The treatment and strategic goals were developed to facilitate therapeutic outcome by maximizing therapeutic leverage while minimizing the influence of previous perpetuants and other forms of resistance to change.

Treatment consisted of a trial of serotonergic antidepressant that would be minimally stimulating. Outpatient sessions with the psychiatrist, 20 minutes weekly, focused on symptom reduction and returning to work. This meant that some collaboration with C. W.'s supervisor about work and peer support was initiated. The supervisor agreed that C. W. needed a familiar, trusting social support, and was able to assign one of C. W.'s coworkers to the same office to which C. W. had been moved. An initial treatment agreement was established for six 45-minute sessions combining medication and interpersonal therapy. They also agreed that skill-oriented group therapy was probably the treatment of choice for C. W. to increase trustability and decrease her social isolation. Aware that C. W.'s pattern of avoidance would make entry into and continuation with the group difficult, the plan was for the individual sessions to serve as a transition into group, after which shorter individual sessions would focus on medication management, probably on a monthly and then bi-monthly basis.

Aware of her pattern, the psychiatrist anticipated that C. W. would "test" the psychiatrist and group therapist's trustability and criticalness. Throughout treatment, both clinicians continued to be mindful of the therapeutic leverage (success with nicotine abstinence, relations with cousin and pet, and with the close-knit typing pool) as well as of the perpetuants that would likely hamper treatment.

4

The Consultor Role Function

Now having considered the evaluator and provider role functions, we turn our attention to the consultor role function. The designation "consultor" is used because it is more inclusive than the term "consultant." Consultor encompasses a variety of functions including consultation, supervision, team leader, collaborator, and advocate. This chapter focuses largely on the consultor role function with regard to the collaboration among prescribing clinician, nonmedical therapist, and patient. Highlighted are strategies for increasing collaboration among these three parties, and common legal considerations in this collaboration.

As noted earlier, the consultor role function shares commonalities (that is, plan, pattern, and prognosis) with the evaluator and provider roles. However, there are notable differences as well. First, in the consultor role function the psychiatrist may have little or no face-to-face contact with the patient, and instead interfaces with a nonmedical therapist and, occasionally, nonpsychiatric physicians. Second, relationships with nonmedical therapists take on different forms with varying degrees of legal liability (Applebaum, 1991).

The American Psychiatric Association (1980) outlines three kinds of relationships between psychiatrists and nonmedical psychotherapists: consultative, collaborative, and supervisory. In the consultative relationship, the psychiatrist has no ongoing relationship with the patient and the therapist is not obliged to follow the psychiatrist's counsel. In the collaborative relationship, responsibility for treatment is shared, such that the psychiatrist is responsible for the patient's medications and physical complaints. Finally, in the supervisory relationship, the psychiatrist actively directs all facets of the nonmedical therapist's work. Applebaum (1991) adds that in the supervisory, as contrasted with the consultative relationship, the nonmedical therapist is obliged to follow the psychiatrist's counsel.

In this chapter, the consultor role encompasses supervisory, consultative, and collaborative relationships, along with a specific oversight function. This contrasts with the traditional psychiatrist role function as supervisor and team leader. Unlike the authoritative, independent role of the past, it emphasizes an interdependent-collaborative relationship with nonmedical therapists, particularly regarding medication and combined treatments.

PHARMACOTHERAPIST–PSYCHOTHERAPIST COLLABORATION

The advent of increasingly effective psychotropic medications with fewer side effects and better safety profiles has led to growing collaboration between nonmedical therapists and prescribing psychiatrists. This collaboration can not only lead to the amelioration of symptoms, but also increase the patient's availability for and capacity to respond to psychotherapy. However, efforts to collaborate can confuse, complicate, and even sabotage both treatments. The addition of a second professional in the treatment matrix can engender negative transference as well as problematic countertransference (Busch & Gould, 1993).

This can occur because the collaborating clinicians tend to have a different treatment focus and goals, and relate to the patient differently in terms of duration and frequency of sessions. While the prescribing psychiatrist may be principally focused on managing relationships with the patient and psychotherapist to maximize medication compliance and hopefully increase a positive placebo response (Spiro, 1986), the nonmedical therapist is principally focused on enhancing the patient's self-management and interpersonal relationships functioning. Furthermore, the two collaborators usually differ in gender, age, interpersonal style, professional discipline, and attitudes toward somatic and psychosocial therapies. Not surprisingly, projective identification and splitting can be expected.

Projective identification refers to the patient disavowing unacceptable parts of the self and attributing them to one of the clinicians, who begins to behave as if the patient's attributions were true. In splitting, this projective process extends so that one clinician becomes idealized and feels compelled to nurture and protect the patient while the other clinician is devalued and feels like attacking or rejecting the patient. If not carefully managed, splitting can sabotage the treatment process. Early signs of splitting include distorted perceptions, such as idealization or devaluation of the other clinician. When splitting is present, coordination of treatment with the other clinician becomes crucial. Both must be willing to step back and clarify the perception of each other that the patient has presented. Then, they must be able to present a "unified front" to the patient, supporting the other's treatment approach and each other in interactions with the patient. If necessary, they see the patient conjointly until a resolution of the splitting is achieved (Woodward, Duckworth, & Guthiel, 1993).

It is for such reasons that some caution against "overly close collaboration" between psychiatrists and nonmedical therapists. For instance, Kelly (1992) insists that frequent communication between clinicians and the sharing of impressions about the patient's problems and progress toward treatment goals can be destructive to treatment. Kelly believes this can engender unacknowledged and unchecked competition between the clinicians, as well as infantilizing the patient. Instead, he proposes that the prescribing psychiatrist relate to the nonmedical therapist as a consultant rather than as a collaborator or supervisor, since he doesn't believe real collaboration is possible when individuals are trained in nonmedical disciplines.

On the other hand, many others (Beitman, 1991; Blackwell & Schmidt, 1992; Busch & Gould, 1993) advocate collaboration. When the roles of both clinicians are clearly distinguished, frequent discussions about the patient and treatment goals can facilitate treatment outcome. In fact, Busch and Gould (1993), a psychiatrist and a social worker who routinely collaborate, find that the quality of collaboration is crucial to treatment outcome. They indicate that mutual respect, trust, and openness are necessary in developing an effective collaboration. They point out that collaborative communication can be quite useful to both clinicians if they sensitize each other to their concerns. For instance, because the nonprescribing clinician sees the patient more frequently, he or she should be able to recognize early signs of hypomania in a patient who is taking an antimanic medication. Or, the prescribing clinician, concerned that a patient's inability might be a side effect of fluoxetine, can learn from the other clinician that the patient is usually irritable without the medication.

THREE-WAY THERAPEUTIC CONTRACT

Several authors (Applebaum, 1991; Beitman, 1993a; Chiles et al., 1991) have extended the discussion of collaboration between prescribing clinician and nonprescribing clinician to include the patient. They recognize that a three-way therapeutic agreement must be reached covering the purpose of each treatment, the clinicians' roles, the patient's role with each clinician, frequency and duration of sessions, policies for communication between the clinicians, any supervision of one clinician by the other, arrangements for emergencies and coverage after hours, and exceptions to confidentiality of records. This agreement should be summarized in writing.

The frequency of collaboration in a managed care setting is largely influenced by practice guidelines. At a minimum, it should occur at the beginning and end of treatment, when problems arise, or when major changes in medication or treatment modalities occur, or at times when either clinician is unavailable because of vacation or sick leave (Woodward, Duckworth, & Guthiel, 1993). In short, it is important that pharmacotherapists and psychotherapists clarify their roles, responsibilities and relationships to assure that patients are appropriately served and the risks for the clinicians are minimized.

Training psychiatrists for these consultor role functions will facilitate the adoption of these role functions (Blackwell & Schmidt, 1992; Kay, 1991; Sabin, 1991; Sabin & Borus, 1992). Kay (1991) believes that future psychiatrists will receive training to teach and supervise other health care personnel, as well as in leadership and administrative skills. Woodward et. al. (1993) contend that psychiatric residency and other professional training programs should include explicit training in pharmacotherapist-psychotherapist collaboration.

GUIDELINES FOR PHARMACOTHERAPIST–PSYCHOTHERAPIST COLLABORATION

1. Before referral is initiated the psychotherapist should establish a working relationship with a "compatible" pharmacotherapist. Areas to be discussed include the specifics of collaboration: indications for referral; arranging the three-way treatment agreement;

policies for communication; coverage for weekends, evenings, vacations, and emergencies, etc. Similarly, the pharmacotherapist should develop a relationship with "compatible" psychotherapists for referring patients for concurrent psychotherapy.

2. During the course of evaluating any new patients, the psychotherapist should consider indications for medical evaluation, medication evaluation, or other concurrent combined treatment. This possibility should be routinely discussed with the patient at the outset of treatment. Similarly, the pharmacotherapist should consider the indication for combined treatment in the initial medication evaluation session.
3. When a patient is deemed appropriate for medication consultation, the psychotherapist prepares the patient for concurrent treatment. This usually involves reviewing the treatment agreement and describing the purpose for the consultation, and the nature of the three-way treatment agreement among patient, psychotherapist, and pharmacotherapist, especially the role and expectations of each. This discussion should be documented in writing in the patient's chart.
4. The psychotherapist then contacts the pharmacotherapist about the consultation request and presents relevant history. The pharmacotherapist provides an initial impression and the psychotherapist documents the conversation.
5. During the medication consultation, the patient is evaluated and, if indicated, a medication trial is discussed with the patient. Combined treatment is discussed in terms of treatment method, duration, the manner of relating to both clinicians, and especially, the matter of coverage for emergencies. Documentation of informed consent and the particulars of the concurrent medication protocol are documented in the patient's record by the pharmacotherapist. A consultation report is sent to the psychotherapist.
6. Thereafter, the pharmacotherapist contacts the psychotherapist and discusses the patient's response to the medication trial(s). The essentials of this conversation are documented by both clinicians.
7. The psychotherapist discusses the consultation results with the patient and reviews the three-way treatment agreement, particularly regarding communication and coverage. This is documented.
8. During the course of combined, collaborative treatment, both clinicians ask the patient about progress of the other treatment, and

encourage compliance/adherence. Both clinicians confer about progress and problems, particularly issues of "splitting" and any changes in treatment plan. Both document such conversations.

9. Finally, when one of the treatments is stopped, the clinicians confer on progress and outcomes. This is documented. The treatment agreement for the ongoing, single treatment is then reviewed with the patient and documented.

LEGAL CONSIDERATIONS IN COLLABORATION

Since medication has demonstrated effectiveness in a variety of psychiatric conditions, the matter of pharmacotherapy needs to be addressed in the evaluation of all patients presenting for psychotherapy. Not to do so may constitute malpractice as in the ruling on the Osheroff vs. Chestnut Lodge lawsuit (Klerman, 1990). Of the many legal issues in pharmacotherapist-psychotherapist collaboration, confidentiality, informed consent, and malpractice liability are particularly important.

Confidentiality is the obligation to safeguard from third parties material that is shared in the professional setting. The central problem in confidentiality cases is surprise, i.e., someone unexpected is found to have confidential information about the patient. Not surprisingly, feelings of betrayal, suspiciousness, and litigiousness often follow this discovery. Woodward et al. (1993) note that preparation is the key remedy for the problem of surprise. This means that an explicit and careful explanation of what becomes of information discussed in the course of treatment should occur at the beginning of the professional relationship. It also means a reviewing with the patient of all documents that leave the office and an anticipatory discussion regarding unavoidable breaches of confidentiality. In collaborative treatment, the issue of confidentiality arises when the patient is surprised and becomes distressed that one clinician knows something that has been disclosed to the other, or in clinical emergencies, when the psychotherapist calls the pharmacotherapist regarding hospitalization of a suicidal patient.

Informed consent extends beyond the prescription of medication for a patient to two other circumstances. The first involves the need for discussion of the risks and benefits of psychotherapy. This should include expectations for therapy, fees, scheduling, and coverage for emergencies. This discussion, including the patient's response, should be documented in a progress note (Applebaum & Guthiel, 1991). The second involves discussion of the roles of both collaborative clinicians at the outset of treatment and thereafter as often as necessary.

Malpractice occurs when there is negligence or breach of a duty of professional care. Pharmacotherapists may be liable for negligence in prescribing, but can be also be held liable for "negligent supervision" if their supervision of the collaborating psychotherapist is below the standard for the practice of supervision. The pharmacotherapist might also be "vicariously liable" for the actions of those they supervise or employ (Woodward et al., 1993).

THE CASE OF C. W. (Continued)

The initial treatment plan for C. W. involved the combined modalities of medication management and a short course in interpersonal psychotherapy for depression, with gradual transition into a time-limited group therapy focused on interpersonal skill development. As C. W.'s depressive symptoms ameliorated and a maintenance medication schedule was established, the psychiatrist began preparing C. W. for transition into the group. Because of C. W.'s fear and ambivalence of the group process, the psychiatrist suggested and C. W. agreed that it might be helpful to meet with the therapist leading the interpersonal skills group C. W. was slated to join. During their fifth session, the group therapist was briefly introduced to C. W. and discussion of a three-way treatment agreement ensued. The three agreed that C. W. would continue in individual weekly appointments concurrent with weekly group sessions. Assuming things were proceeding well enough, sessions with the prescribing psychiatrist would be reduced to monthly medication checks.

A subsequent two-way discussion between therapist and psychiatrist concluded that there was little likelihood that projective identification and splitting would be issues with C. W. Instead, difficulty maintaining active group participation and follow-up on "homework" between group sessions were predicted. The psychiatrist agreed to encourage and support the patient's group involvement in his concurrent individual sessions with C. W. Furthermore, the therapist and psychiatrist planned on conferring after the third group session regarding the transition from weekly to monthly sessions with the psychiatrist.

CONCLUDING COMMENTS

The identities and roles of mental health professionals will continue to evolve in the coming years. It has been my purpose here to overview the nature of these changes, particularly as they impact the psychiatrist practicing in a managed care setting. I have proposed a specific role for the psychiatrist to match the psychiatrist's unique training, values, and biopsychosocial perspective, as well as the values and demands of managed care. The role involves a collaborative leadership relationship with other health and mental health personnel for the purpose of maximizing psychotherapeutic and psychopharmacological outcomes. Table 2 compares this role and role function with previous ones.

This role and the functions of evaluator, provider, and consultor require a somewhat different leadership style, as well as a focus on treatment outcome rather than on treatment and service delivery per se. Nevertheless, I am hopeful that psychiatrists can be trained to ef-

TABLE 2
Role Functions with Differing Role Definitions for the Psychiatrist

Authoritative/Independent Leadership	*Supportive/Subordinate Position*	*Collaborative Leadership*
expert diagnostician		principal **evaluator**
differential therapy prescriber		differential therapy **evaluator**/prescriber
psychosocial therapy provider		focused combined treatment **provider**
somatic therapy prescriber/provider	somatic therapy prescriber/provider/referrer	somatic therapy prescriber/**provider**
medical evaluator/provider/referrer		medical **evaluator/provider**/referrer
treatment team leader and supervisor	"sign off" supervision	treatment team **consultor**: (supervisor, consultant, oversight function)

fectively collaborate with other mental health professionals to provide state-of-the-art, combined treatments that are both cost-effective and efficacious. For not to prepare, educate, and mentor psychiatrists and psychiatrists-in-training about evolving roles in managed care "is to fail in our responsibility to the future of psychiatry" (Lewis & Blotcky, 1993, p. 192).

Part II

General Treatment Strategies and Guidelines

5

Combining Treatment Modalities

There has been increasing interest in combined therapies, tailoring, and integrative treatments. This follows a long period of time in which clinicians were skeptical or even hostile about combining two modalities like individual psychotherapy and group therapy, or medication and psychoanalytic psychotherapy. The question of combining psychotherapy and psychopharmacology was first debated at a major conference at McGill University in 1958. It was attended both by noted psychoanalysts and psychopharmacologists. Many attendees rejected the prevalent psychoanalytic view that medication had no specific curative effects, but simply reinforced powerful transference and countertransference feelings. In 1962, Ostow's classic monograph, *Drugs in Psychoanalysis and Psychotherapy*, was published, and in the 1970's amid the emergence of a number of research studies on combined treatments the Committee on Research of the Group for the Advancement of Psychiatry published *Pharmacotherapy and Psychotherapy: Paradoxes, Problems and Progress* (1975). Of these early studies, the most notable was that by Rounsaville, Klerman, and Weissman (1981) in which the long-standing belief that medication interfered with psychotherapy was not empirically supported. Rather, it was documented that both treatments are complementary. Karasu's (1982) analysis of several research studies concluded that psychotherapy treated "traits" while medication treated "state" symptoms.

Klerman (1986) extensively reviewed all existing research on combined treatment and found that combined treatment tended to have an additive or synergistic effect, but most often there was some effect. The majority of studies of combined modalities have been focused on depression. For the most part, these studies have shown some modest advantage of combined treatment over individual treatment both in terms of acute and long-term efficacy (Fava & Kaji, 1994; Hollon & Fawcett, 1995).

So what is combined treatment and is it now related to tailoring and integrated treatment? Let us begin with tailoring. Tailoring refers to modifying or adapting a particular modality and/or therapeutic approach to the patient's needs, styles, and expectations.

A sartorial analogy might help distinguish combining, integrating, and tailoring. An adult could go into a clothing store to purchase a grey business suit. The individual could randomly choose a suit from the rack. There is a small chance it would fit perfectly, but more likely it will be a less than perfect fit. The individual whose size is usually 38 short could look through the racks and try on 38 short, which might fit quite well but needs some minor fitting work by a tailor–*partial* tailoring, of course. The individual could also go to a store for a fitting and have a suit completely custom made–*total* tailoring. Now the suit could be pure wool or pure silk, or it could be a blend of wool and silk. This blended fabric would be analogous to integrating treatment. Analogous to combined treatment, would be the purchase of a blue sports jacket that might be worn with the slacks of the grey suit for a more casual look (Sperry, 1995).

In short, combined treatment refers to *adding* modalities, such as individual, group, couple, or family, either concurrently or sequentially, while integrative treatment refers to the *blending* of different treatment approaches or orientation, such as psychodynamic, cognitive, behavioral, interpersonal, etc. Combining treatment modalities is also referred to as multimodal treatment. Finally, tailored treatment refers to specific ways of customizing treatment modalities and/or therapeutic approaches to "fit" the unique needs, cognitive and emotional styles, and treatment expectations of the patient.

Once considered controversial, psychoanalytically oriented therapy combined with other modalities is now being advocated by dynamically oriented clinicians. Winer and Pollock (1989) indicate that combined treatment: insight-oriented individual sessions with medication, group, or family therapy is particularly valuable in cases of personality disorders.

Treatment delivered in combination can have an additive, and sometimes synergistic, effect. It is becoming more evident that different treatment approaches are differentially effective in resolving different types of symptom clusters. For example in major depression, medication is more effective in remitting vegetative symptoms, while psychotherapy is better at improving interpersonal relations and cognitive symptoms (Frances, Clarkin, & Perry, 1984). Furthermore, the additive effect of medication and psychotherapy has been established for both major depression (Rush & Hollon, 1991) and agoraphobia (Greist & Jefferson, 1992).

While combined treatment refers to combining different modalities of treatment (i.e. individual group, marital, and family therapy, day treatment, or inpatient) either concurrently or sequentially, integrative or tailoring treatment is different. Integrative treatment refers to blending various treatment approaches (i.e., psychodynamic, cognitive, behavioral, interpersonal, and medication). Recently, several therapists have advocated integrative treatment for borderline personality disorder (Stone, 1993; Linehan, Heard, & Armstrong, 1993). Cognitive behavior therapy represents the integration of two therapeutic approaches: cognitive therapy and behavior therapy. The specific type of cognitive-behavior therapy developed by Linehan, dialectical behavior therapy, is an integration of various cognitive-behavioral intervention strategies and Zen practice (Heard & Linehan, 1994). Stone (1993) prescribes blending psychoanalytic, behavioral, cognitive, and medication interventions or approaches.

What are the indications and contraindications and treatment guidelines for these various modalities? Unfortunately, these questions cannot presently be answered with the kind of research-based clinical precision that clinicians and utilization reviewers typically want. For now, this chapter translates and extends the best available clinical research data regarding these questions. The following sections describe specific indications, contraindications, and treatment guidelines for combining individual therapy and medication group therapy and medication, family therapy and medication, individual and family therapy, and individual and group therapy. First, a prerequisite treatment guideline for combined treatment must be mentioned.

PREREQUISITE GUIDELINE FOR COMBINED TREATMENT

Perform a detailed pragmatic assessment of the outcomes of combined treatment based on: (1) the patient's treatability; (2) availability of provider expertise and the capacity for effective collaboration among providers; and (3) the cost effectiveness. In addition to the information provided by a complete traditional evaluation, this assessment specifies the severity and chronicity of the condition, the patient's expectation for treatment outcome and involvement in treatment, previous successes and failures in various changes outside psychiatric treatment, and previous history of noncompliance and relapse/recurrence in psychiatric treatment. In short, this is the patient's potential for treatability. Chapter 2 discusses the concept of assessing treatability.

Effective collaboration between and among competent providers is multifaceted and complex. Were there only transference and countertransference issues, the managing of splitting and projective identification would be a challenge, but a reasonable challenge. However, there are also a number of complex, legal issues in collaborative professional relationships, such as confidentiality, informed consent, and malpractice, which also must be addressed. Chapter 4 discusses a number of these matters.

Finally, the question of cost-benefit needs to be part of the decision to offer or continue combined treatment. Specifically, the question to be answered is: Will the proposed combined modalities provide the best qualitative and long-lasting results and are they affordable as compared to other treatment, or even no treatment, options?

COMBINING INDIVIDUAL PSYCHOTHERAPY AND PSYCHOPHARMACOLOGY

Of all the combined treatments, combining individual psychotherapy and psychopharmacology is the oldest, the most described, and the most widely practiced. But it is not always clear where psychopharmacology ends and psychotherapy begins. Fawcett and colleagues (1987) described an approach to medication management that is largely supportive in nature and, while sharing commonalities with nonspecific approaches to psychotherapy, is not specifically psychotherapy. Rather consistently, studies have shown that patients treated with medication and some form of individual therapy–be it psychodynamic, behavioral, or cognitive–show at least modest improvement than patients given medication alone. Whether the effect is additive or synergistic, the combined treatment mode affects both biological and psychosocial diatheses. Thus, while an anxiolytic may suppress panic attacks, individual psychotherapeutic interventions reduce phobic avoidance. And, where a neuroleptic suppresses delusions and hallucinations, individual psychosocial interventions encourage socialization and facilitate reality testing. The end result is that patients who are less anxious and depressed and are better able to concentrate have been forced to be more accessible to psychological interventions and, subsequently, lead better and more productive lives (Karasu, 1982).

Because of the rapidly expanding literature on combining various individual interventions with medication for the various Axis I and II diagnostic categories, this section won't provide general indications, contraindications, and treatment guidelines as for the other combined treatment modes. Instead, these specific guidelines and strategies will be provided for specific diagnostic categories in Part IV and for inpatient treatment and geriatric patients in Part IV.

COMBINED GROUP THERAPY AND PSYCHOPHARMACOLOGY

Combining group intervention with medication is one of the more common combined treatment modes. More than two thirds of group therapists surveyed recently reported that medicated patients were members of their outpatient psychotherapy groups (Stone, Rodenhauser, & Markert, 1991). The most common diagnosis of these patients was mood disorders, followed by personality disorders, anxiety disorders, and schizophrenia. It should be noted that this study did not survey group therapists involved with the increasing number of medicated patients in skill-oriented groups, rehabilitation groups, or medication groups in day hospitals or outpatient clinics. Group therapy is particularly effective in improving self-esteem, modulating emotional reactions, and developing appropriate interpersonal and social skills. On the other hand, medication can ameliorate anxious, depressive, manic, psychotic, and disorganized thinking and suppress pathological ruminations, compulsions, and impulsivity (Sussman, 1993).

Psychotropic medications have greatly expanded the population for whom group therapy is now available and have also expanded the theory and practice of group therapy itself. Other survey data suggest that dynamically oriented group therapists have been slower in their acceptance of this treatment combination than group therapists of other orientations (Rodenhauser & Stone, 1993). Finally, this combined treatment has broader applicability than combined family therapy and psychopharmacology, since not all patients have families that are available and willing to participate in the treatment process.

Indications and Contraindications

This form of combined treatment is indicated in at least four instances: (1) to ensure medication compliance; (2) to increase the patient's social skills and/or social involvement; (3) as an adjunct or the main focus of aftercare treatment following discharge from an inpatient treatment setting. In all of these three instances, combining group with medication is indicated. A fourth indication is when symptoms interfere with patients' involvement in a group in which they are already members. This is less common than the first three indications. Nonetheless, medication can greatly ameliorate certain target symptoms, allowing the patient to be more emotionally accessible to the therapeutic process of the group. There are relatively fewer contrain-dications for this combined mode than for combining individual and group therapy, since patients treated for certain target symptoms–impulsivity, aggressivity, extreme hypersensitivity, and the like–may become more accessible to psychological intervention. However, patients with untreated or partially treated psychosis or mania may be too disruptive for such groups until their symptoms are better modulated. Linehan (1987) reports that lower-functioning, chronically parasuicidal patients diagnosed with borderline personality disorder can respond to structured group therapy.

SPECIFIC TREATMENT GUIDELINES

Prior to initiating the combined format, the clinician should perform a comprehensive evaluation of the patient in terms of Axis I and II diagnosis, level of functioning, social and interpersonal skills, extent of social support network, target symptoms, and indications for combined group therapy and psychopharmacology.

The group therapy format includes heterogeneous and homogeneous groups (Frances, Clarkin, & Perry, 1984). Heterogeneous groups tend to be comprised of patients who differ widely in presenting diagnosis, target symptoms, level of functioning, socioeconomic status, and personality style. Heterogeneous groups are also characterized by their focus on interpersonal relations in a wide variety of contexts and tend to be ongoing, open-ended groups where members can join and "graduate" at various points. Homogeneous groups, on the other hand, tend to be composed of patients with similar diagnoses. For example, an eating disorder group or a medication symptom management group is a homogeneous group. These groups are more likely to focus on a specific target symptom and condition, to be more directive than heterogeneous groups, and to be time-limited rather than long-term and ongoing.

The following are some points to consider when combining medication with group treatment.

1. Refer lower functioning patients with medication-modifiable target symptoms and/or noncompliance/ nonadherence issues to homogeneous combined treatment groups, and higher functioning patients on medication who have minimal social skills to a heterogenous group.

Generally, homogeneous groups are better suited to patients with chronic medication noncompliance or other nonadherence issues who have difficulty in social functioning and/or experience persistent symptoms, such as dysphoria, anxiety, referential thinking, or hallucinations. These patients may be a good "fit" for a medication and/or symptom management group. Protocols for medication and symptom management groups are described in Chapter 7.

On the other hand, heterogeneous groups may be more appropriate to higher-functioning patients on medication whose trait symptoms are well controlled and who have at least minimal social skills. Not surprisingly, heterogeneous groups are more likely to be found in private practice and other outpatient settings. Accordingly, not all patients in heterogeneous groups will be on medication and issues of medication noncompliance may not likely be a common topic of discussion. However, issues about the meaning of medication and the fantasies associated could be the focus of discussions. Some patients on medication may resist discussing medications, while others will openly flaunt their medication and the "specialness" of having a "real" doctor–the prescriber–also caring for them (Rodenhauser & Stone, 1993). Fantasies of being controlled or losing control because of medication may be reflected in resistance to group process. Similarly, problems regarding intimacy are often projected onto the medication themselves (Zaslav & Kalb, 1989).

2. Usually, psychopharmacology precedes the introduction of group therapy.

Most often acute target symptoms preclude the patient's accessibility to the therapeutic process–whether individual or group–and so medications are usually begun first. Whether the referral is for a heterogeneous or homogenous group, the patient must be relatively stable. Some patients, particularly those who are exceedingly shy or dependent, may need to be gradually introduced into the group modality. Thus, a few individual sessions may be necessary to encourage and socialize the patient to make the transition to the group modality. Sometimes, a few concurrent individual and group sessions are needed before the prescribing clinician is able to reduce individual sessions to a medication-monitoring mode.

3. Attend to the potential collaboration issues.

Despite the encouraging finding of the Rodenhauser and Stone (1993) and Stone, Rodenhauser, and Markert (1991) studies about the increasing acceptance of medicated patients in groups run by nonprescribing clinicians, there is considerable potential for splitting and countertransference. The conduct of group therapy and the management of medication both require considerable expertise. Clinicians in both instances need to appreciate the therapeutic potential as well as adverse reactions attendant to this combined treatment (Sussman, 1993). Although the prescribing clinician may be involved in a medication- management group, a symptom-management group, or other homogeneous group, it is quite unlikely that the prescribing clinician will be leading a heterogeneous group. Therefore, issues of collaboration can be paramount. Ideally, the prescribing clinician can refer medicated patients only to groups and group therapists sharing similar views about this combined treatment and having a previous track record of working collaboratively with medicated patients. When this is not possible, it is the prescribing clinician's responsibility to assess the potential group therapist's attitudes about medication and receptivity to collaborative relationships, which can be expected to be fraught with splitting and projective identification. Specific guidelines for pharmacotherapist-psychotherapist collaboration are provided in Chapter 4 of this book.

COMBINING FAMILY THERAPY AND PSYCHOPHARMACOLOGY

The first generation of controlled studies of the efficacy of combined family therapy and medication is currently underway. Although largely focused on schizophrenia, some trials have studied combined treatment of mood and eating disorders, as well as of panic disorders and agoraphobia. This type of combined treatment is particularly valuable in suppressing symptoms, educating the family about the psychiatric disorder, improving family communication and problem-solving skills, and resolving dynamic and systems issues created by the disorder (Glick, Clarkin, & Goldsmith, 1993). This section briefly describes medications/contraindications and two treatment guidelines.

Indications and Contraindications

This combined treatment is indicated for many instances of both specific symptoms of an individual family member and the family problems and interactions that accompany these conditions. Specific indications are: (1) to enhance medication compliance; (2) amelioration psychiatric symptoms of the identified patient that delimit or preclude full participation in a family therapy; and (3) to reduce relapse and recurrence of the psychiatric disorder. An obvious contraindication is when either of the two modalities is in itself effective. A relative contraindication includes previous failure or current stalemate in family therapy.

SPECIFIC TREATMENT GUIDELINES

Prior to initiating the combined treatment format, the clinician must make both a DSM-IV diagnosis and a family systems diagnosis (Beavers & Hampson, 1990). Without such a combined diagnostic formulation, neither the appropriate medication nor family intervention(s) will be prescribed or implemented. Furthermore, the clinician must be aware of the side effects of the medication and the family therapy, as well as their interaction (Glick, Clarkin, & Goldsmith, 1993).

Following are some guidelines for this combined format:

1. Set specific outcome goals, particularly regarding target symptoms, for both modalities, based on which symptoms are medication responsive and which are family-intervention responsive.

Without such a delineation of target symptoms, it may be impossible to determine which modality–or combination–is effective. Typically, these target symptoms are disabling anxiety, vegetative symptoms of depression, positive symptoms of schizophrenia, impulsivity, aggressivity, and affective instability.

2. Initiate treatment with the medication modality and add the family modality when the patient is stabilized.

This guideline is applicable will hold for the majority of patients who are experiencing acute, debilitating psychiatric symptoms. For example, the psychotic patient who is paranoid may not be able to tolerate family sessions until stabilized by medication. Before that, the patient might be too suspicious of the clinician or of other family members to benefit from treatment.

COMBINING INDIVIDUAL PSYCHOTHERAPY AND FAMILY THERAPY

Individual psychopathology and family dysfunction are nearly always interdependent. Interpersonal and intrapsychic dynamics reciprocally interact between each person and his/her family and social contexts. Various clinical reports and research studies combining individual therapy with either marital or family therapy have been published since 1966. This section describes five indications for this format and three treatment guidelines. Obviously, the combined treatment assumes that the individual family of origin or nuclear family are available and willing to be involved in treatment.

Indications and Contraindications

This combined treatment is indicated when the presenting problems include one or more of the following: (1) an adult whose symptoms are being triggered or reinforced by marital or family dysfunction; (2) a highly pathological level of marital discord; (3) sexual dysfunction; (4) a child or adolescent with a psychiatric disorder or significant symptom; and (5) a highly pathological level of parent-child conflict (Sanders & Feldman, 1993).

Relative contraindications for this combined format include: (1) the adult's presenting problem does not have a significant etiology in or effect upon the family system; or (2) strong motivation to be seen alone, such as adolescents who insist they have personal problems for which they will seek only individual help.

SPECIFIC TREATMENT GUIDELINES

Individual and family modalities can be combined in two different ways. Either treatment can shift sequentially from one modality to the other or the two modalities can occur concurrently. Feldman (1992) describes sequential integration and "concurrent" integration, which can be either symmetrical–equal emphasis on each modality–or asymmetrical–emphasis on one modality over the other. Sanders and Feldman (1993) advocate that the same clinician provide both modalities. However, two clinicians may be better utilized in the following circumstances: (1) an individual therapy relationship has been firmly established prior to the plan to add marital or family therapy; (2) the number or severity of the presenting problems is usually high; and (3) a family member is extremely resistant to "sharing" his or her therapist with other family members.

Following are some specific guidelines:

1. When the presenting complaints are predominantly interpersonal, begin with marital or family therapy. When the presenting complaint is predominantly intrapsychic, begin with individual therapy; afterwards, the other modality is added.

This is the sequential strategy and is more commonly employed than the concurrent strategy. In utilizing the sequential strategy, marital or family therapy is more often added to individual therapy than vice versa (Sanders & Feldman, 1993).

2. When the degree of individual and family interactional dysfunction is equally high and there is little resistance to either modality, begin both concurrently.

This is the symmetrical, concurrent strategy. With couples, this means the partners are seen conjointly one week and then individually the next. In conjoint session, they work out relational issues, while treatment in individual sessions focuses on dysfunctional cognitions, family of origin issues, or intrapsychic dynamics. With families, the entire family has a conjoint session and later that week the identified patient has an individual session (Sanders & Feldman, 1993).

3. When family interactional dysfunction is manifestly greater than intrapsychic dysfunction, or vice versa, or there is a great resistance to individual sessions, begin with primary emphasis on the modality not resisted. Later, the others may be added.

This is the asymmetrical, concurrent strategy. Assuming that both modalities are being utilized, the primary modality is scheduled weekly, while the secondary modality might be biweekly or monthly (Sanders & Feldman, 1993).

COMBINING INDIVIDUAL PSYCHOTHERAPY AND GROUP THERAPY

Combined individual and group therapy is one of the oldest and most effective of all treatment combinations. While often considered simply an amalgam of individual and group therapy, it is a separate approach in its own right. It has its unique indications and contraindications, mechanisms of action, and technical issues (Porter, 1993). Over 100 publications on this combined format have appeared since 1949. This section will briefly describe mechanisms of action, indications-contraindications, and general treatment guidelines.

The mechanism of action of this combined format has both additive and magnifying effects for both individual therapy and group therapy. Porter (1993) notes that additive effects for individual therapy include one-to-one corrective emotional experiences and deep intrapsychic exploration. Additive effects for group therapy include the exploration of multiple transferences and provision of a context in which to risk new behaviors. The magnifying effects of adding individual therapy include prevention of premature dropout from group therapy, and in-depth exploration of material from group sessions. Magnifying effects of adding group therapy include prevention of premature dropout from individual therapy and analysis of transference resistance from individual sessions.

Indications/Contraindications

The consensus on this combined format is that it is appropriate and may be the outpatient treatment of choice for: (1) personality disorders–except the antisocial and severe narcissistic, borderline, paranoid, schizoid, and schizotypal personality disorders; (2) most impulse control, sexual, and substance abuse disorders; (3) most mood and anxiety disorders; and (4) stable psychotic conditions. Specific contraindications are acutely suicidal individuals, those who are extremely shy, those with focal neurotic symptoms who have no personality disorders, and patients for whom combined treatment is a resistance to treatment already occurring (Porter, 1993).

SPECIFIC TREATMENT GUIDELINES

Combined individual and group therapy can be initiated in three ways: (1) beginning with individual and then adding group therapy; (2) beginning with group and then adding individual therapy; or (3) simultaneously initiating both modalities. Generally, the third option is uncommon. Similarly, this combined format can be ended in three ways: (1) terminating individual before group therapy; (2) terminating group before individual; or (3) terminating both simultaneously. Commonly, the two modalities are provided by different clinicians. When two clinicians are involved, the issue of collaboration between group therapist and individual therapist in terms of goals and focus must be negotiated. This issue of collaboration has been discussed in general terms in Chapter 4. Lipsius (1991) offers four specific guidelines to achieve a balance as well as to maximize the synergy between the two modalities.

1. Start individual therapy for most patients and then add the group component.

The exceptions to this guideline are patients who have an intense fear of close one-to-one relationships and need the anonymity of a therapeutic group as a prerequisite to individual therapy, as well as those with a long history of previous individual therapies with limited results.

2. When appropriate, invite the patient to relate individual and group session material and assist with interpretations that are helpful in integrating the patient's therapeutic experience.

Specifically, Lipsius (1991) suggests that both clinicians inquire if what the patient experiences in one treatment modality relates to what he or she is experiencing in the other modality. He believes that this approach identifies intermodality resistances, which when resolved result in the vital process integration of previously incompatible parts of the self. Moreover, it prevents premature termination of either or both modalities.

Transference splitting is the main technical issue faced in this combined format. Common among patients with dependent and histrionic styles is positive transference in individual sessions counterbalanced with negative affect in the group setting. Among patients with schizoid and paranoid styles, the reverse is common. Porter (1993) contends that the presence of transference splitting represents the emergence of a tendency that otherwise might erupt outside the treatment setting with greater self-destructive consequences. He recommends supporting these patients in fully expressing their feelings in whatever modality they appear. The absence of certain feelings in the other modality can then be addressed, which initiates a process of reversing the split and facilitating integration.

3. Terminate the individual modality before the group modality.

There are a few exceptions to this general guideline: when difficulty with separation is the central issue, ending both modalities simultaneously is preferable for patients whose treatment is reasonably complete. Terminating group therapy first is preferable when the patient has completed much in the combined modalities but still experiences transference difficulties within the individual modality (Porter, 1993).

OTHER COMBINED TREATMENT MODES

While combining two treatment modalities may be sufficient for many patients and circumstances, there are other patients and circumstances in which three or more modalities may need to be combined. The most common of such combined modes involves individual therapy, medication, and either group or family sessions. At this time, there has been very little written or researched on such multiple combined modalities to offer specific indications or guidelines. Occasionally, in the following chapters, such multiple combined treatment will be mentioned.

6

Ensuring Medication Compliance and Treatment Adherence

The ultimate goal of clinician-patient interaction is to ensure that effective treatment occurs. Effective treatment outcomes are, in large part, a function of treatment compliance. Compliance refers to how faithfully a patient follows the advice and direction of the clinician (Sperry, 1985). Poor compliance is a major problem in health care, particularly with psychiatric patients. In a general setting, one study showed that one third of patients complied with all treatment recommendations, one-third complied with some recommendations, and one-third were completely noncompliant (Sackett & Haynes, 1976). When medication is prescribed to patients without current symptoms, or to prevent recurrence of symptoms, the rate of noncompliance is about 50 percent. However, for those with diagnoses of schizophrenia and/or personality disorder, compliance is even worse (Docherty, 1988)!

Recently, the term *compliance* has acquired a pejorative connotation implying a passive and subservient patient in relation to an active, authoritarian clinician. As a result, the term *adherence* has become the preferred designation with most treatment regimens (Sperry, 1985). Although drug or medication adherence is used by some, most continue to favor the designation *medication compliance* (Blackwell, 1976). In this chapter, compliance refers to medication treatment, while treatment adherence will refer to all other treatment regimens.

The key variables known to affect compliance include patient factors, clinician-patient interaction, the treatment regimen itself, and family factors. This chapter overviews each of these four variables and suggests treatment guidelines to enhance compliance and adherence. Since the patient's spouse and family can significantly influence compliance and adherence, family factors and guidelines for "family compliance counseling" (Doherty & Baird, 1984) are emphasized.

PATIENT FACTORS

1. Assess relevant patient characteristics: stages of change, explanatory model, and personality style.

Three patient characteristics that have been shown to predict compliance/adherence are readiness or stage of change, belief and explanatory index, and personality styles (Beitman, 1993b; Docherty, 1988; Ward, 1991).

Readiness or **stages of change** refer to a normative, sequential way for conceptualizing both the duration and outcome of treatment (Steenbarger, 1994). Patients who change their behavior move through a series of stages from "precontemplation" to "contemplation" to "action," and then to "maintenance" (Prochaska & DiClemente, 1984). Chapter 2 describes these stages of change. How is this readiness for change or stages of change measured? By interview and observation, or by the 32-item Stages of Change Scale (McConnaughy et al., 1989).

Eliciting the patient's **explanatory model** of his/her illness and related beliefs is essential to both establishing a collaborative relationship and ensuring compliance/adherence. The patient's explanatory model or formulation of why he or she is ill and symptomatic can be fraught with misinformation or misattribution. Such "explanations" become the basis for patient education and negotiation. For instance, bipolar patients who believe that their illness was caused by insomnia and can be cured by a good night's sleep need to have their "explanation" corrected by educating them about the biopsychosocial aspects of bipolar disorder. Similarly, the patient who explains her generalized anxiety in terms of a single early life trauma should hear the clinician describe a more complete model of the illness that also allows for her particular concerns about the early trauma. Specific irrational beliefs about illness or treatment must also be elicited and addressed.

The delusional belief that the medication to be prescribed is a poison is one obvious example. A less obvious irrational belief involves patients with low self-esteem. They may ascribe negative meaning to medication, viewing it as representative of their personal deficiency or worthlessness. This projected badness can then be externalized and dismissed by refusal to accept the medication that will protect them from further loss of self-esteem (Docherty, 1988).

Helping patients understand their illness is best done in a biopsychosocial context, particularly for those patients seeking a magic pill (Ward, 1991). Negotiated explanations that are tailored to the patient's experience are particularly valuable. Such explanations should be simple, integrate biological and psychosocial mechanisms, and incorporate some elements of the patient's explanation. For example, a schizophrenic patient may be helped to accept that he has a biochemical imbalance that leaves him overly reactive to his environment and other people–the perceptual filter model of psychosis–resulting in social withdrawal and simple phobia. Or, the patient insisting that hypoglycemia is the basis for his major depressive episode might be offered a treatment plan in which blood glucose would be measured immediately and reevaluated if a four-week trial of medication is not successful (Ward, 1991).

Finally, medication can be perceived as both a vehicle and agent of control. It may be viewed as a chemical means by which the clinician exerts control over the patient's thought or action. Thus, the patient's noncompliance is a means of controlling and defeating the clinician. Similarly, noncompliance may function as a projective identification, as when the patient's feelings of helplessness are projected onto and induced in the clinician.

How are irrational beliefs and explanatory models assessed? The clinician should inquire about the patient's meaning and explanation of illness, symptoms, and susceptibility to illness. Furthermore, the clinician needs to know the patient's specific fantasies about the medication and its effects. Finally, the clinician needs to elicit the patient's beliefs about the benefits of treatment, especially how the financial, social and psychological costs of the treatment will influence the patient's compliance and adherence (Docherty, 1988).

Since **personality style** reflects persistent and predictable patterns of perceiving, thinking, feeling, and acting, a knowledge of the patient's personality style or dominant traits can be useful in the understanding and interpretation of patterns of compliance and noncompliance. For instance, since dependent patients often want to be liked and accepted by their clinician, they may take the medication to please the clinician. Dependent patients can be the clinician's most compliant patients. On the other hand, they may graciously agree to take the medication and report taking it when in fact they are not. Generally, this is because the medication is inconsistent with their explanatory model, or they cannot afford it, or taking it would displease a family member or significant other. Occasionally, a dependent patient taking medication will fail to report or deny side effects, not wanting to displease or risk the possibility of being rejected by the clinician "for complaining."

Compulsive and paranoid patients often require extensive details and explanation regarding their treatment in order to be reassured. Although they expect their clinician to be an expert, they are likely to be more compliant when they are offered a number of options and thus believe they have some measure of control over their treatment. For instance, a paranoid patient may balk at taking a fixed dose of a neuroleptic. However, the patient may have a better response and be more compliant if he can titrate the dose (Ward, 1991).

Passive aggressive and hostile dependent patients are particularly prone to partial compliance and noncompliance. It has been said that these patients are more interested in defeating clinicians than in getting better. Such patients may demand detailed explanation and rationales for a proposed treatment regimen and then refuse that medication on some related technicality. If they do take the medication they have been shown to report more adverse side effects than other patients, even when they have been given placebos! Such patients should be counseled that a positive treatment outcome cannot be guaranteed and that the best that can be offered is an attempt at treatment. Difficulties and side effects should be presented in a matter-of-fact fashion when a predictive interpretation about expected side effects is made. To the extent to which these patients must defeat their clinician, they will likely prove the clinician wrong by minimizing any such side effect (Ward, 1991).

In short, knowledge of a patient's personality style can be useful in enhancing compliance and adherence. Thus, the clinician should pay particular attention to Axis II disorders and traits. The computer-generated reports by NCS for the Millon Clinical Multiaxial Inventory (MCMI) can be particularly useful in assessing personality style dimensions.

2. Modify the treatment regimen–clarify, simplify, and tailor–to effect better compliance.

There is overwhelming evidence that complex treatment regimens–multiple medications prescribed or given in divided doses–adversely affect medication compliance (Blackwell, 1976). Compliance can be greatly enhanced when the treatment regimen is clarified, simplified, and tailored.

Clarify the treatment regimen: It is preferable for patients to receive both oral and written instruction detailing the dose and dosing schedule, as well as the usefulness of this drug for their psychiatric disorder. Misperceptions and misunderstanding can be easily checked if, after receiving the instructions, patients are asked to tell the clinician what they understand about how the treatment regimen works and why it is being prescribed.

Simplify the treatment regimen: Attempt to decrease the number of daily administrations to the minimum. Patients have a far easier time with once-a-day dosing whenever it is possible. While most neuroleptics and antidepressants lend themselves to q.d. dosing, it may be possible with select patients to prescribe lithium and other antimanics on a q.d. basis. Consider the use of long-acting intramuscularly administered agents, such as depot haloperidol and fluphenazine, for those patients who have difficulty complying with an oral dosing regimen.

Tailor the treatment regimen: Tailoring refers to individualizing or customizing information and scheduling to the patient's personality style and circumstances. With regard to personality style, paranoid and compulsive patients need more detailed information about treatment regimen than dependent and histrionic patients. While depressed compulsive patients may be told they will be started on an antidepressant that takes 3–4 weeks to reach optimal effect and that they have a 70 percent chance of responding favorably to a drug that reverses depressive symptoms but is non-addicting, histrionic patients are better told that they will be feeling better in 3–4 weeks and their sleep should improve even sooner. Any specific concerns and fears of histrionic patients should be handled as they appear. Similarly, the manic who endlessly describes "cosmic consciousness" may refuse an antimanic if it is prescribed "for mood swings." However, that patient might be more willing to comply with the medication if it is prescribed "to help you focus and center better" (Ward, 1991).

In addition, the regimen should be tailored to the patient's life circumstance. Specifically, medication compliance is increased when medication taking is incorporated into the patient's current daily routine. For instance, doses arranged around daily self-care rituals such as at a specific meal or at bedtime.

3. Enhance collaboration between clinician and patient to optimize compliance/adherence.

Not only compliance but also the therapeutic effects of medication are enhanced when patients have a working, collaborating relationship with a clinician who is concerned and positive (Blackwell, 1976; Ward, 1991). Collaboration can be enhanced in at least two ways: by tailoring the nature of the relationship and by triggering the placebo effect.

Tailoring the nature of the relationship: How the clinician relates to the patient depends on the patient's diagnosis, degree of impairment, and personality style. The clinician must decide how much dependence to allow the patient, as well as how much authority to exert. With more impaired patients, the collaboration between clinician and patient will be more dependent than with less impaired patients who are capable of more autonomy and are willing to use it. Similarly, the clinician must also decide the extent of warmth and intimacy the patient can tolerate. While histrionic and dependent patients respond to warmth, paranoid, and schizophrenic patients tend to distrust it. As the patient improves, the clinician must be prepared to shift the relationship. So, as the patient gains more autonomy, the clinician must allow the patient a wider range of choices and decisions.

Triggering the placebo effect: Placebo effect is that part of improvement resulting from nonspecific factors, such as hope, suggestion, expectancy, or "explanations" of the problem, that reassure the patient (Walrond-Skinner, 1986). It is instructive to note that placebo response rate in drug trials varies with diagnosis. Patients with generalized anxiety disorders most frequently respond to placebo–about 50 percent–while those with obsessive compulsive disorders have a lower rate–from 0 to 20 percent (Beitman, 1993b). While a convincing explanation and mechanism of action for placebo response has yet to be articulated, the placebo effect is a reality and potentially is present in all clinical situations. This effect can and should be utilized to enhance the benefit of the prescribed medication or other treatment.

The placebo effect not only enhances the relationship between clinician and patient, it also increases compliance and adherence (Ward, 1991). The clinician can enhance the placebo effect in several ways: by spending time with the patient, by expressing interest and concern, and by demonstrating a confident, professional manner. In the initial phase of treatment, more frequent face-to-face encounters with the patient have been known to increase the placebo effect. As treatment proceeds and the patient improves, follow up appointments can be scheduled less often and should be framed to the patient as opportunities to monitoring continued progress (Shapiro & Morris, 1978).

Quitkin et al. (1993a) found that a considerable portion of patients relapsed in the first three months of antidepressant treatment and that this was due to loss of placebo effect. Patients who were placebo responders were those who had abrupt versus gradual onset of improvement and were more likely to relapse. This phenomenon is discussed in more detail in Chapter 8, Preventing Relapse and Recurrence. For now, a clinician dealing with such a situation can reassure patients that they may have actually improved through their own resources and that a different class of antidepressant will be tried (Quitkin et al., 1993b).

FAMILY FACTORS

The patient's spouse or family can greatly influence medication compliance and treatment adherence. For instance, husbands with highly supportive wives were significantly more likely to comply with medication regiments than those with less supportive wives. Supportive spousal behaviors that enhanced compliance were "reminders" and "encouragement," while nonsupportive behaviors were "nagging" and "lack of concern" (Sackett & Haynes, 1976). Psychiatric patients are more prone to have some disturbance of the marital or family system (Beavers, 1985). This disturbance can take many forms. Among these are beliefs antithetical to the conduct of treatment, overt or covert efforts to undermine treatment, and lack of external monitoring of the patient's behavior and adherence to the treatment regimen (Docherty, 1988).

A family system view of medication compliance and treatment compliance has been described by Doherty and Baird (1984). It involves a therapeutic triangle consisting of the clinician, the patient, and the patient's family. Compliance involves the cooperative efforts from which the patient derives the resources, support, and information necessary to adhere to the agreed-upon treatment regimen. Four factors are necessary for the therapeutic triangle to enhance compliance. First, there must be congruence in expectations and belief related to the psychiatric disorder and treatment. In other words, the patient and the family must acknowledge and accept the diagnosis and need for treatment. Second, the clinician and the family must know how to support the patient's attempts to comply with the regimen. Third, the clinician and the family must be sufficiently motivated to provide such support. And, fourth, the clinician and the family must provide sufficient support. Doherty and Baird (1984) have also described a compliance protocol.

The following are treatment recommendations/strategies for utilizing the family to enhance medication compliance and treatment adherence.

1. **Utilize family compliance counseling when indicated.** Indications for family compliance counseling include patients with chronic psychiatric conditions such as schizophrenia, bipolar disorders, or personality disorders, particularly patients with previous treatment failures, refractory symptoms, or repeated recurrences.
2. **Follow the family compliance counseling protocol, adapting and tailoring it to a given patient and family.**
   a. **Arrange for a family session or at least a session with one family member.** Even in the most pathological family, at least one family member has a good relationship with the patient and appears genuinely concerned about the patient's health and well-being. Asking the patient if such an individual exists is usually the most accurate and direct way of identifying such an ally (Ward, 1991). When there is less family pathology, it is valuable to include as many members as possible. Ideally, the clinician encourages the patient to bring family members to the next session after the diagnostic and treatment formulation are agreed upon. Patients generally accept the rationale that the clinician needs to explain matters to the spouse or family members and to respond to their concerns and questions. If the family has previously subverted treatment because certain or all family members are more invested in control and keeping things the same rather

than in the patient's welfare, family therapy should be considered (Ward, 1991; Goldstein, 1991).

b. **Start the family session with a discussion of the psychiatric disorder and the proposed treatment.** The advantage of communicating this information directly to the family is that they can receive the information undistorted by the patient's anxiety or misunderstanding. This is the first step in forging a therapeutic alliance with the family regarding the treatment plan.

c. **Next, elicit questions and reactions from the patient and family members.** Ask first for reactions or questions about the diagnostic treatment formulation, and then about their reactions to and acceptance of the patient's psychiatric illness. If the family has difficulty accepting the patient's psychiatric disorder, the clinician must not proceed with treatment until acceptance is achieved.

d. **Then, shift to a problem-solving mode by helping the family and patient establish an agreement about compliance with the prescribed regimen.** The goal is to establish a supportive family interaction pattern. Begin by asking the patient if he or she would like other family members' help in following through with the treatment regimen. If the patient responds affirmatively, ask a family member whether he or she would agree to assist the patient. Assuming the family member–for instance, the spouse–agrees, the clinician says he would like them to plan a way that they would work together on compliance. The clinician's role is to teach and guide them in the skill of behavioral contracting. It is essential that the patient ask for support, while remaining responsible for his or her own compliance behavior.

e. **Distribute any material, particularly handouts about the prescribed medication. Ask everyone to read and become familiar with the material.**

f. **Schedule and conduct a follow-up family session to monitor progress of treatment and the effectiveness of the family support contracts made during the prior family session.** The family's behavioral contract may need to be modified and updated. The clinician helps with this and encourages them to continue their efforts. If long-term treatment is envisioned, periodic booster sessions, perhaps every three to six months, may be scheduled.

CONCLUDING NOTE

In summary, the following are treatment guidelines for enhancing medication compliance and treatment adherence:

1. **Assess relevant patient characteristics: stage of change, explanatory model, and personality style.**
2. **Modify the treatment regimen to effect better compliance.**
3. **Enhance collaboration between clinician and patient to optimize compliance/adherence.**
4. **Consider involving the family or spouse.**
5. **If the family is involved, follow the family compliance protocol.**

7

Incorporating Psychoeducational Strategies

Psychoeducation is a broad term that encompasses any educational experience that meets a patient's specific learning needs, interests, and capabilities. It is a communication activity that occurs within the clinician/patient encounter and influences patient behavior toward improved functioning and well-being. Psychoeducation includes a variety of strategies designed not only to facilitate behavior, such as increased medication compliance, but also to help patients and their families to identify their social support network and maintain their achieved behavior over an extended period of time.

Psychoeducation is more than a medication information sheet or watching a video clip on recovery from a depressive episode. That "more" is a personal interaction between clinician and patient that instills hope and establishes an expectation for change and commitment to that change. The purpose of psychoeducation is to provide patients and their families with enough information and motivation to help themselves understand the factor that promotes and/or threatens mental health, so that they may have a better opportunity to make informed choices. In addition, it provides the technical assistance and support necessary to help patients carry out their choices (Lewis, Sperry, & Carlson, 1993).

TYPES OF PSYCHOEDUCATION

There are different types of psychoeducation that are useful in the treatment of psychiatric patients. These are patient education, patient handouts, self-help organizations, medication groups, and related social skills training. Each of these types will be briefly described, while medication groups and symptom management strategies will be described in more detail.

Patient Education

While inpatient and day treatment programs traditionally include formal patient education, activities in outpatient clinic settings can also effectively include formal patient education activities as part of a comprehensive treatment plan. Patient education programming can easily be incorporated in outpatient settings in small instructional groups that include patient and/or family. A number of training materials and lesson plans in such topics as: "What Is Mental Illness," "Medication to Treat Mental Illness," "Decreasing Your Chance of Relapse," "Hazards of Substance Abuse," "Coping with Your Symptoms," and "Family Interaction" are available, as are a number of audiovisual aids, including related videotapes. Bisbee's (1991) *Educating Patients and Families About Mental Illness* is among the best of such resources. It has lesson plans, handouts, transparencies, and a listing of readily available videotapes for the patient education and family education programs. A number of short videos that are quite valuable learning tools are available gratis from drug companies. For instance, Sandoz has a 13-minute video called "What to Expect," describing the use of clozapine. The National Mental Health Association and Eli Lilly have a 15-minute video on depression called "Moving Back to the Light," with a clinician's and a patient's education guide. Such videos can be viewed by the patient at either the clinic or at home and discussed in a subsequent session.

Patient Handouts and Bibliotherapy

The most common form of psychoeducation is the patient handout. It is usually a simple one- or two-page information sheet that is either commercially available or adapted from any number of sources. Wyatt (1994) has developed an outstanding collection of handouts for patients and their families, covering all the major psychiatric disorders, and all the major classes of medication. Two versions of each medication sheet are available: a short 2-page version that is concise and easy to read, and a more detailed 6-page version for patients or family members who want or need additional information.

A number of excellent booklets have been developed by the American Psychiatric Association (APA), the National Alliance for the Mentally Ill, and the Dean Foundation. The APA's "Let's Talk About Mental Illness Series" has brief pamphlets on depression, bipolar disorder, schizophrenia, and substance abuse, to name a few. An appendix in Bisbee (1991) lists several more handouts and audiovisual materials and the sources for securing these materials. Greist and Jefferson have authored an excellent series of short books (30–50 pages long) that are quite valuable with higher functioning, better educated patients and their families. Six titles are currently available. These include "Antipsychotic Medication and Schizophrenia," "Carbamezapine and Manic Depression," "Electroconvulsant Therapy," "Lithium and Manic Depression," "Obsessive Compulsive Disorder," "Stimulants and Hyperactive Children." These booklets are available from the Dean Foundation: 800 Excelsior Drive, Madison, Wisconsin 53717-1914.

Bibliotherapy refers to the use of written material, such as self-help books, that aid patients in altering their behavior, thoughts and feelings. Unlike patient handouts material that serves to inform, bibliotherapy serves to assist the change process of psychotherapy. These materials, used properly, can be a potent adjunct to psychotherapy. For example, reading Lewisohn et al.'s (1978) self-help book *Control Your Depression* has been shown to be as effective in reducing the symptoms of mild to moderate depression as formal individual or group psychotherapy (Brown & Lewisohn, 1984). There are a number of highly regarded self-help books that clinicians prescribe as an adjunct to therapy. Some of the better known are David Burns' *Feeling Good: The New Mood Therapy* (Signet, 1980) and Claire Weekes' *Peace From Nervous Suffering* (Bantam, 1978). *The Authoritative Guide to Self-Help Books* (Santrock et al., 1994) is a clinician's resource book on using bibliotherapy with psychiatric patients. It provides a detailed evaluation of 500 self-help books.

Self-Help Organizations and Support Groups

Self-help organizations are a third form of psychoeducation that outpatient clinicians can incorporate in a comprehensive treatment plan.

Patients with a particular condition or problem can be referred to a growing number of groups that share information or provide mutual support. These groups are often led by nonprofessionals, although professionals may be invited to present a topic for discussion at a meeting of the support group. Recovery, Inc. and the National Depressive and Manic Depressive Association are established self-help organizations that have support groups in most communities in North America. Several other groups have come into being recently, many based on the 12-step model, including AA, NA, ACOA, etc. Support groups for obsessive compulsive disorder, panic and agoraphobia, and other specific psychiatric disorders may also be recommended as adjuncts to professional clinical treatment.

MEDICATION GROUPS

Medication groups are another type of psychoeducation that is particularly targeted to chronically mentally ill patients. Although these groups can have a variety of treatment formats and protocols they all share similar goals. These goals are: increased knowledge about medication and its effects, enhanced medication compliance and other treatment adherence, and increased socialization and support.

Medication groups typically meet weekly to monthly for 45 to 90 minutes. These groups are usually clinic-based and may be held prior to or following an individual appointment with a mental health clinician, or they may be the only mode of psychiatric treatment. The groups usually are led by one to three clinicians, with from eight to 15 patients in attendance. Usually, one is a prescribing clinician. The other clinician(s) may be a nurse, social worker, or psychologist. Medication groups are mostly homogeneous groups, meaning that a group consists of individuals with similar disorders, such as schizophrenia or mood disorders, or with similar classes of medication, such as neuroleptics or antidepressants or antimanics. Medication groups can range from being relatively unstructured–wherein any concerns about medication, diagnosis, other treatments, or personal issues can be discussed–to quite structured, with scheduled presentations or specified topics for discussion. Some medication groups follow a manualized skills training format that is time-limited (Liberman, 1986).

Are medication groups effective? To date, there has been little controlled research reported on the efficacy of medication, except for studies by Frank, Kupfer, Perel, et al (1990) and on Liberman's manualized skill training program. Non-controlled studies reported by Masnik et al. (1980), Moffic (1982), and Shakir et al. (1979) showed decreased rehospitalization rates, decreased amounts of medication prescribed, and increased medication compliance and other treatment adherence. Davenport et al. (1976) reported on medication groups for bipolar patients on lithium carbonate that also involved spouses. As compared to patients followed up for individual medication monitoring, the couples medication group had fewer rehospitalizations, better medication compliance, and higher social functioning and family interaction. Evaluation of Liberman's medication management skills training program with 160 schizophrenic patients showed increased medication compliance, increased knowledge of medication use, and increased use of medication management skills (Eckman & Liberman, 1990a; b). Dekle and Christensen (1990) found that patients who completed such medication management program(s) were more likely to keep appointments and to effectively negotiate medication issues than patients provided standard treatment.

Indications and Contraindications

The main indications for candidates for long-term medication groups are chronic psychiatric patients with diagnosis of schizophrenia, bipolar disorder, major depression, or schizoaffective disorder who need education about their illness and medications, compliance enhancement, and/or social support and socialization. Contraindications are active suicidality, severe substance abuse and/or dependance, violent behavior or a history of disruptive behavior in groups, acute psychosis, and dementia (Brock, 1993).

TREATMENT GUIDELINES FOR MEDICATION GROUPS

Assuming the patient is appropriate for medication group treatment, the following treatment guidelines are offered.

1. **Prepare the patient for entry and participation in the group.**
   In one or two individual sessions, the patient is socialized in the manner in which the medication group will function. First, reasons for referral and the benefits of the group are presented and discussed sufficiently so that mutual agreement about group medication monitoring is achieved. Second, the therapeutic contract is discussed. This usually includes matters of confidentiality, the availability of individual sessions at times of crisis if the group is the only source of treatment, and the kind of collaboration between medication group clinicians and other treatment providers. Third, instructions regarding appropriate group participation are given.
2. **Make individual sessions available during periods of decompensation or stressful life circumstances.**
   Since medication groups are the sole source of psychiatric treatment for many chronic patients, it is necessary, as well as cost-effective, to provide limited concurrent individual sessions with one of the group leaders while the patient weathers a psychiatric episode or other severe stressor.
3. **Utilize group process dynamics appropriately given the level of treatability of group members.**
   Medication groups are not simply educational courses, but derive their therapeutic efficacy from such group process dynamics as instillation of hope, universality, imitative behavior, identification, and group cohesiveness, in addition to support, safety, continuity, and imparting of information and skill learning (Vinagradov & Yalom, 1989). These groups provide a supportive setting to deal with issues that positively or negatively affect the use of medication. Lesser and Friedmann (1980) contend that not all chronic patients are so brittle that discussion must be kept at a superficial level as was once previously believed.

There are various medication group formats. The decision about format should match patient need, staff expertise, and clinic treatment philosophy. Diamond and Little (1984) describe two different medication groups operating concurrently in a mental health clinic. Both groups have a drop-in format that meets weekly one hour. One has an unstructured format, while the other has a schedule of lectures and discussion topics determined both by group members and leaders. Brook (1993) described a scheduled one-hour weekly format to which some 60 patients are assigned, but patients are expected to attend only once every three or four weeks. The format is flexible and determined by the leaders. Shakir et al. (1979) describe a 75-minute weekly group format for recently discharged bipolar disordered patients that has a here-and-now, interpersonal focus (Yalom, 1985) in which issues range from medication side effects to loss and dependency feelings. Members are expected to attend weekly, but cut back to monthly attendance after returning to full-time employment.

Finally, Liberman's (1986) manualized medication management skill training program is mentioned again. This program can stand on its own, meeting for 12 weekly sessions and then terminating, or it could be incorporated in part or fully in an ongoing medication group format. Although originally produced for schizophrenic patients, this program appears equally useful for all major Axis I disorders. The program involves the following skill areas: obtaining information about medication; knowing correct self-administration and evaluation of medication; identifying medication side effects; and negotiating medication issues with clinicians. Learning activities in each skill area include videotapes, role plays, in vivo exercises, and homework assignments.

SYMPTOM MANAGEMENT TRAINING

Many patients with chronic psychiatric disorders experience hallucinations, severe dysphoria, paranoid ideation, debilitating anxiety, or periods of confused and disorganized thinking. These symptoms provide patients in a group with a common topic for discussion, and members can reality test each other's unusual experience or empathize with a member's mood instability. For instance, if a patient reports auditory hallucination, others can reassure that patient that they do not hear the same voice, and suggesting that while the experiences may seem real, the voices are not real. The group leader can assess this symptom and help the group to differentiate acute from warning and persistent symptoms, as well as discuss strategies for coping with such symptoms. Patients can then share various techniques they have found useful in coping with *persistent symptoms* (for example, chronic, low-grade symptoms not ameliorated by medication), *warning symptoms* (for example, symptoms gradually increasing in intensity that precede an acute episode), or *acute symptoms* (for example, the full-blown incapacitating symptoms that signal acute decompensation) (Liberman, 1988). Since acute and warning symptoms can result from insufficient medication levels or noncompliance, it is usually reasonable to raise medication levels or add an additional agent. On the other hand, persistent symptoms do not usually suggest insufficient medication levels or noncompliance and thus do not require changing dosage or drug regimen; psychosocial intervention–particularly distraction techniques and strategies–is the treatment of choice. While symptom management can be accomplished in individual sessions, group sessions can be a particularly effective treatment format.

An awareness and understanding of these three types of symptoms is a prerequisite for preventing relapse, which often means rehospitalization for both acute and chronic psychiatric patients. Liberman (1988) has developed a skill training program for managing symptoms. This program involves four skill areas: identifying warning symptoms of relapse; managing warning symptoms; coping with persistent symptoms; and avoiding alcohol and street drugs. Like the medication management program, the symptom management program consists of several learning activities and formats: videotapes, role plays, and in vivo exercise and homework assignments. This program can stand alone as a time-limited group that nearly all psychiatric patients could profit from. Furthermore, parts of this program can also be incorporated into an ongoing medication group.

Indications and Contraindications for Symptom Management Training

Any patient with residual or persistent symptoms that are relatively unchecked by medication is a candidate for this form of psychoeducation. This includes patients who regularly ask or demand medication changes, with the expectation that the "right" medications at the "right" dose will "solve" all or most of their problems. If symptom management is done in group format, the same relative contraindications for medication groups apply.

The reader is referred to the Trainer's Manual for Liberman's *Symptom Management Module* (1988) for specific treatment protocols and guidelines, and to the text by Liberman, De Risi, & Meuser (1989) for general background information on social skills training with psychiatric patients.

8

Preventing Relapse and Recurrence

Webster's defines relapse as the recurrence of symptoms of a disease after a period of improvement. Klerman (1978) and Frank, Prien, Jarrett, et al. (1991) have attempted to differentiate relapse from recurrence. They designate relapse as a continuation of the "original" episode and recurrence as the instigation of a "new" episode. While it may be useful and necessary to differentiate relapse and recovery in research protocol and studies, in clinical practice the distinction is purely academic. For the purpose of this book, both terms will be used synonymously.

Currently, it appears that patients with diagnoses such as schizophrenia, depression, bipolar disorder, and addictions are more likely to relapse than patients with other disorders. But while it is possible to predict the types of disorders and, to some extent, identify individuals with that disorder who are more prone to relapse, it is not possible to predict the timing or severity of the relapse (Wilson, 1992). This chapter describes the biopsychosocial components of relapse and then provides three treatment guidelines regarding relapse and its prevention.

BIOPSYCHOSOCIAL COMPONENTS OF RELAPSE

Most patients experience a relapse or recurrence of symptoms and other aspects of a disorder because of a combination of biological, psychological, and social factors or determinants. Relapse is conceptualized somewhat differently by psychologists and psychiatrists. Psychologists like Marlatt (Marlatt & Gordon, 1985) describe relapse from a psychosocial perspective: being in a high-risk situation with limited coping skills and a decreased sense of self-efficacy, along with a perceived loss of control, leads to relapse. High-risk situations are those that pose a threat to the patient's sense of control and increase the risk of potential relapse. Marlatt and Gordon (1985) report that the majority of relapses in adults occur in high-stress situations involving negative emotional states, interpersonal conflict, or social pressure. The extent to which the patient is unable to cope effectively in a high-risk situation and has little expectation of being able to master the situation increases the probability of relapse.

This perspective has little room for the biological. On the other hand, psychiatric literature has focused almost entirely on biological factors (Klerman, 1978; Quitkin et al., 1993). However, recent findings from the NIMH Treatment of Depression Collaborative Research Program (Elkin, 1994) lend strong support to a biopsychosocial view of relapse and relapse prevention. That research program and others have combined pharmacotherapy with psychotherapy, either cognitive therapy or interpersonal psychotherapy, and have concluded that combined treatment offers the best long-term prophylaxis against relapse. Interestingly, Fava and Kaji (1994) conclude that studies of cognitive therapy alone show that it has efficacy in relapse prevention, defined as prophylaxis for less than one year, while interpersonal psychotherapy has efficiency in recurrence prevention, defined as prophylaxis for greater than one year.

GUIDELINES FOR PREVENTING RELAPSE AND RECURRENCE

1. Assess the patient's potential for relapse and recurrence.

Earlier in this chapter mention was made that predicting who will relapse, when, and how severe the extent of relapse is far from being an exact science. There are some limited data on predictors of relapse. For example, Kavanaugh (1992) reports that high levels of expressed emotion, i.e. intrusive behavior of either moderate to severe environmental stressors, and being male with an early age of onset are predictors of relapse in schizophrenics. Fava and Kaji (1994) note that certain patients are at risk for relapse and recurrence of a Major Depressive Episode. Seven predictors are given: (1) chronicity and a highly recurrent course of depression, i.e., three or more episodes or those with major depression superimposed in dysthymia; (2) a long duration of the first episodes prior to treatment; (3) the presence of persistent residual depressive symptoms at the end of acute treatment; (4) being single; (5) greater dysfunctional attitude and more negative self-appraisal; (6) younger age; and (7) high degree of neuroticism and personality disorder or traits.

Unfortunately, these data do not reflect the timing of relapse, in other words, changes in the patient's status during and after the course of treatment that led to relapse. Further research may provide a more complete profile of relapse potential, but for the present time a detailed clinical assessment is indicated. Wilson (1992) proposes that prediction can be made from the patient's history, status at pretreatment, responsivity during treatment, status at post-treatment, and status during follow-up. The clinician would do well to consider the following factors in estimating relapse potential:

a. **Patient's history:** This should include the duration of the disorder; precipitants, including number and type of life event stressor, social support network, number of episodes of the disorder, age, gender, and socioeconomic status.
b. **Status at pretreatment:** This would include type and severity of symptomology, status and Global Assessment of Functioning (GAF), cognitive style, expectations for treatment outcomes, and readiness for change.
c. **Treatment response:** This would include the following: medication compliance and treatment adherence, such as keeping appointments, doing homework, etc.; responsiveness to medication–i.e., true drug effect vs. placebo effect; quality of therapeutic alliance; the patient's responsiveness to relapse prevention procedures; and the presence or absence of persistent symptoms.
d. **Status at post-treatment:** This would include mental status, degree of improvement in daily functioning, i.e., GAF, presence of persistent symptoms, and after-care plan for relapse prevention.
e. **Status during follow-up period:** Occurrence and reaction to life events, social support network, medication compliance

and/or continued adherence to treatment strategies, and relapse prevention plan.

While the clinician may only be able to collect data on patients' history and pretreatment status on new patients, the overall relapse prevention strategy being proposed here assumes that as treatment proceeds, the clinician can be sensitized to other potential indicators of relapse.

From my clinical experience, I have been impressed with the predictiveness of the following indicators of relapse:

- Presence of persistent symptoms
- Precontemplation or contemplation stage of change
- Minimal or inconsistent social support network
- Absence of, or noncompliance with, a relapse prevention plan
- Placebo-response effect to medication or psychotherapy (flight into health or transference cure)

Regarding the matter of placebo response effect to medication, it might be said that the placebo effect is quite common in both controlled drug trials and clinical practice. It has been shown that the placebo response varies for different diagnoses, with the largest response–50 percent–in patients with diagnosis of generalized anxiety disorder. Those with obsessive compulsive disorder have very low placebo response rates–less than 20 percent. Suggestibility or low expectation for change are hypothesized for these variations in placebo response (Beitman, 1993b).

Whatever the explanation, clinicians need to be aware that the placebo effect can account for relapse and recurrence in the acute phase of pharmacologic treatment. Quitkin et al. (1993) report that relapse can be predicted in patients on antidepressants based on the speed, timing, and persistence of improvement. Invariably, those patients who responded abruptly within two weeks of starting the medication relapsed. In contrast to these placebo responders, those patients who had a gradual and delayed onset of improvement, taking more than two weeks, and persisting thereafter, were considered to have a true drug effect. The clinical implication is that the clinician who recognizes an abrupt onset and a fluctuating course should anticipate that such patients have a greater chance of relapsing and thus require greater surveillance. Furthermore, the clinician can reassure patients discouraged by the apparent loss of drug benefits that they may have actually improved through their own resources and can encourage them to try a different class of antidepressant. On the other hand, when relapse has occurred much later in the course of treatment, the patient might instead be treated with an augmentation strategy, such as adding lithium, thyroid, or amphetamine (Quitkin et al., 1993).

2. Consider the impact of personality style on relapse.

Personality style clearly influences how a person perceives, thinks, feels, and acts; therefore it will impact relapse and recurrence in a predictable pattern. This section briefly describes patterns of relapse for various personality styles.

Dependent tendencies make it difficult for patients to reach decisions, assert themselves, and take responsibility for their actions. Since therapy involves increased independence and emotional risk-taking, dependent patients are ill-equipped to manage themselves outside of their closest relationships. They find the solo effort and energy involved with making these internal changes so daunting and frightening that they tend to increase the demands they place on others to take responsibility for their decisions and feelings of impotence. As they become aware of the limits that others place on these dependency demands, they become more vulnerable to relapse.

Passive-aggressive tendencies lead patients to express anger indirectly by shifting blame, complaining, procrastinating, and making excuses. When faced with the openness and directness that therapy requires, these patients tend to feel threatened. They begin to avoid treatment sessions or those who are trying to help them. Then, alone with feelings of frustration and pessimism, their risk for relapse increases.

Narcissistic tendencies lead patients to view themselves as highly talented and desirable persons. They feel entitled to special recognition, special dispensation, and unconditional acceptance. Thus, they find it difficult to accept constructive feedback or go beyond superficial relationships. Assuming they stay in treatment, they are vulnerable to relapse when they overestimate their progress in treatment and underestimate the severity of their problems.

Obsessive compulsive tendencies lead patients to be perfectionistic, indecisive, inflexible, and emotionally inexpressive. These traits make it difficult for them to organize their feelings and focus on the basic tasks of therapy: let down their guard, risk showing warmth and tender feelings, and admit their humanness. However, even after they have made considerable progress in therapy, minor challenges and stressors can easily send them back into their compulsivity.

Antisocial tendencies lead patients to resist societal norms, rules, and obligations, and to control others through manipulation or aggression. Often, these patients are impulsive and thrill-seeking. Their vulnerability to relapse increases when they reject help from others and try unsuccessfully to control their impulses and cravings for power and stimulation on their own.

3. Integrate relapse prevention strategies into treatment.

A number of different relapse prevention strategies are applicable to various psychiatric as well as addictive disorders (Marlatt & Gordon, 1985; Wilson, 1992). This section describes four: relapse prevention plan, combined treatment and relapse prevention, booster sessions, and minimal contact interventions. Such strategies are best integrated into the initial treatment plan.

Relapse Prevention Plan: Establishing a relapse prevention plan begins at intake with an assessment of the patient's relapse potential. Such a plan involves the clinician and patient working collaboratively to identify four factors: the patient's high-risk circumstances, triggers, thinking errors, and coping-skill deficits. High-risk circumstances are defined as the persons, places, and times of day that are most likely to be experienced as highly stressful. These include such factors as high expressed emotion or intrusive acquaintances or family members, as well as particular times and locations, such as being alone on a Saturday night while family members/or friends are out enjoying themselves. It is also essential that other individuals who maintain and reinforce disorders and symptoms be identified as high-risk circumstance. Triggers refers to negative emotional states, fatigue, cravings for substances, loneliness, hunger, and whatever else may elicit relapse while in high-risk circumstances. Thinking errors refer to negative cognitions or self-talk likely to be triggered in high-risk circumstances. For instance, the patient who is alone on Saturday night and feeling angry and lonely may be thinking that nobody cares about her and that she is a loser because she can't get dates like her friends. As a result, she becomes increasingly anxious and depressed. Coping deficits refer to the absence of coping skills such as lack of assertiveness, difficulties in problem solving or decision making, etc. Continuing with the example, the lonely, anxious, and depressed patient may lack assertiveness in terms of arranging to be with other people socially, and consequently has an increased probability of relapse.

The purpose of such an analysis is to develop a relapse prevention plan that is an antidote for each of the four factors: "alternate circumstances" for "high-risk circumstances," "trigger reducers" for "triggers," "corrective thoughts" for "thinking errors," and "coping behaviors" for "coping deficits." Figure 3 is a worksheet that can be used for this plan.

Combined Treatment and Relapse Prevention: For patients who are receiving medication, combining some forms of psychotherapy, be it family, group, or individual therapy, with medication often provides a prophylaxis against relapse, at least during the course of the combined treatment. This is more likely to be the case when a cognitive-behavioral therapy is employed, since relapse prevention is a core feature of most cognitive-behavioral approaches. For other psychotherapeutic approaches, adding anti-relapse sessions prior to termination of therapy is recommended. For example, Frank et al. (1990) reported that a maintenance form of interpersonal psychotherapy plus imipramine was successful in preventing relapse for three years among patients with recurrent depression.

For combined medication and psychotherapy treatment, the course of concurrent psychotherapy often terminates before medication is discontinued. This is particularly true with depression, bipolar disorder, and schizophrenia, which may require longer-term, even lifelong, medication monitoring. Because the rates of recurrence are relatively high after psychotherapy is stopped, it seems reasonable to continue some psychotherapeutic intervention with a relapse prevention focus throughout the medication on monitoring treatment. The psychotherapeutic focus would concentrate on residual symptoms as well as on dysfunctional attitudes regarding social functioning and medication usage (Fava and Kaji, 1994).

Two excellent reference sources on combined treatment with a relapse prevention focus are Wilson (1992) and Hersen and Ammerman (1994). Because of the importance of preventing relapse and recurrence, Chapters 9–12 will offer specific guidelines regarding relapse prevention.

Booster Sessions: The most common relapse prevention strategy is the booster session, which is the inclusion of additional therapy sessions at some point after the termination of the original treatment program. The content of these sessions is often linked directly to the content of the original treatment, but may involve new techniques that are more specifically designed to prevent relapse.

High-Risk Circumstances (Person, Places, Time)	**Triggers (Feelings, Craving, Fatigue, Hunger, Loneliness, etc.)**	**Thinking Errors**	**Coping Deficits**
1	1	1	1
2	2	2	2
3	3	3	3
4	4	4	4
Alternative Circumstances	**Trigger Reducers**	**Corrective Thoughts**	**Coping Behaviors**
1	1	1	1
2	2	2	2
3	3	3	3
4	4	4	4

Figure 3. Relapse Prevention Worksheet

Most often, booster sessions are scheduled to occur on certain predetermined dates, such as six weeks or six months after terminations. Beutler and Clarkin (1990) suggest that clinicians reestablish contact with patients, and sometimes with their families, on a regular basis. They recommend regularly scheduled appointments at two weeks, one month, three months, six months, and then two years post-treatment anniversaries to facilitate and reinforce prevention efforts. While booster sessions usually involve a face-to-face meeting, planned booster sessions by phone are an alternative if distance or time is an impediment to face-to-face meetings.

Minimal Contact Interventions: These include audiotapes or printed material. This material can be used by the patient on a regular basis. Audiotapes of relaxation instructions have been quite useful for patients with anxiety disorders and insomnia. Similarly, "loop" tapes for response prevention have been quite successful for patients with obsessive thoughts (Salkovskis & Kirk, 1989).

Part III

Specific Treatment Strategies and Guidelines

9

Anxiety Disorders

Anxiety disorders are among the most common presentations treated in outpatient psychiatry. Over the past three decades, our knowledge and skill in treating these disorders have increased dramatically. Whole new disciplines and subspecialties have developed as alternatives to the limitations of the dynamic psychotherapies in treating these disorders. For example, the field of behavior therapy essentially began with efforts to desensitize individuals suffering from various phobias (Wolpe, 1982). In addition, the introduction of meprobamate and other anxiolytics in the 1950's opened new areas in psychopharmacology and brain research. Yet, while the disciplines of behavioral therapy and psychopharmacology seem to be at opposite ends of the mind–brain continuum, there is a significant common link of both theoretical and practical significance. Clinically, this link makes the combined treatment approach for the treatment of the anxiety disorders not only possible but extraordinarily efficacious (Mavissakalian, 1993).

What is this common link? It is desensitization. Desensitization is the common change-producing mechanism in both pharmacotherapy and psychotherapy. Desensitization has been shown to be a common change mechanism in such apparently different psychological approaches as psychoanalysis, existential psychotherapy, and behavior therapy (Beitman & Mooney, 1991). Exposure training is the most potent of the desensitization methods in behavior therapy. In exposure training, patients are asked to face the objects they fear and refrain from using avoidance as their coping mechanism for anxiety. Thus, exposure leads to "learning desensitization." The behavioral learning involves a realization of self-control and reduced likelihood of danger and harm. Similarly, medications lead to "tissue desensitization" in which there is a reduction of responsiveness of neurotransmitters and neural pathways. The concepts of tolerance, habituation, and adaptation are synonymous with tissue desensitization. Medications provide a means for exposure by which these same ideas are learned, but not as effectively as with behavioral exposure. Stopping medication after successful treatment of a panic, agoraphobia, or obsessive compulsive disorder often leads to relapse, which seldom occurs with behavioral exposure. Whereas tissue desensitization leads back to resensitization, learning desensitization through behavioral exposure is essentially irreversible (Beitman & Mooney, 1991). Furthermore, whereas medication quickly results in symptom relief–tissue desensitization–in many anxiety disorders, behavioral exposure–learning desensitization–often takes longer. Thus, there are advantages in combining medication and exposure. Clinical research increasingly supports the combined treatment approach in anxiety disorders (Mavissakalian, 1993).

How effective is treatment of the anxiety disorder? Approximately 25 percent respond to placebo and 50 percent respond well to combined treatment, while the remaining 25 percent do not respond well to the standard strategy of combined treatment (Mavissakalian, 1993). However, the maximizing strategy of integrating more than two treatment modalities leads to increased responsivity.

The following strategies and guidelines reflect the current state-of-the-art in the integrative, combined treatment of the anxiety disorders based largely on reported clinical trials. They are meant to assist the clinician in thinking through treatment decisions, rather than as definitive treatment protocol. Definitive protocol will be available only after considerably more controlled research is reported.

TREATMENT STRATEGIES FOR THE ANXIETY DISORDERS

1. Perform a detailed functional assessment.

Assessment of the anxiety disorder begins in the first session and continues throughout treatment and follow-up. It should be structured and should emphasize functioning in the six P's: presentation, predisposing factors, precipitant, pattern, perpetuants, and prognosis (Sperry et al., 1992). Of these, presentation, pattern, and prognostic factors are the most important for planning treatment.

Presentation: The intensity, duration, and severity of the symptoms should be determined. Intensity can be assessed by helping the patient rate the amount of anxiety experienced on 0-100 scale, with 100 being totally intolerable. This scaling is called "subjective units of distress" (SUDS) (Wolpe, 1982) and is useful in establishing graded hierarchies of the fearful situations avoided by the patient. The severity of the disorder can be estimated by the extent it interferes with daily life, including the ability to work and carry on normal relationships. Begin this inquiry by asking: "What does this anxiety (phobia, compulsion) prevent you from doing?" And "if you no longer had it, how would your life be different?" Of course, duration refers to the length of time that functioning has been impaired.

Pattern: Since avoidance is likely to be a major feature of pattern, detailed information about avoidance is needed. This includes detailing triggering events (physiological, behavioral, and cognitive, i.e., self-talk), and particular factors that make a situation difficult or easy. Determining the full range of avoidance behaviors is useful in drawing up a graduated or hierarchical list of exposure tasks.

Other pattern features are common in anxiety disordered patients, particularly those with panic and/or agoraphobia, or dependency, low self-esteem, and interpersonal sensitivity. Common personality disorders associated with anxiety disorders are dependent, avoidant, and histrionic personality disorders. Approximately 50 percent of patients with panic and agoraphobia meet criteria for one of these personality disorders (Cowley & Roy-Byrne, 1988).

Prognostic Factors: The patient's treatability is related to both functioning, such as the presence of significant personality pathology, and readiness, which includes resources and coping skills as well as realistic expectations for treatment. Personality pathology has significant prognostic implications, in that anxiety disorder patients with personality disorders are less likely to respond to medications or behavioral treatment (Cowley & Roy-Byrne, 1988; Mavissakalian, 1993).

Inquiry about coping methods the patient has tried in the past is useful because those which appear to be adaptive–i.e., distraction strategies such as listening to music or keeping busy–might systematically be incorporated into the treatment plan. The patient's readiness for and capability to collaborate in a treatment is noted by a previous history of successfully tackling difficult situations, changing behaviors such as cessation of smoking, the presence of a supportive social network, and personal characteristics such as persistence and a sense of humor.

Perpetuants: Perpetuants are maintaining factors that interfere with treatment progress. Not surprisingly, avoidance is usually the main perpetuant. A particular individual, such as a spouse who derives secondary gain from the patient's condition, and cognitions involving beliefs about the dangerousness of the phobia or feared object and doubts about the efficacy and outcome of treatment or of the patient's ability to be involved in treatment are also critical factors that must be elicited and considered in treatment planning.

2. Focus treatment outcomes on desensitization.

Tissue and learning desensitization–particularly behavioral exposure–is both the basic treatment strategy and the outcome of treatment. Exposure involves facing the feared object that has been avoided because it provokes fear. Research suggests that for optimal effectiveness exposure should be graded, repeated, and prolonged (Greist, 1992a). Treatment is designed to extinguish anxiety and avoidance responses by exposing patients systematically to feared selections. The clinician's task is twofold–to help the patient design a realistic, graduated exposure hierarchy and, perhaps even more important, to encourage and support the patient in facing the feared object or situation (Butler, 1989). Fortunately, most patients experience relatively little discomfort and anxiety during the course of exposure training, given the length of time they had previously avoided and worried about the things they feared.

Studies show that between 60 and 90 percent of patients with panic and agoraphobia benefit from exposure therapy with a 50 to 80 percent reduction in their symptoms. Some become completely symptom-free, but most have occasional recurrence of symptoms. For that reason, relapse prevention should be a part of treatment (Mavissakalian, 1993).

3. Treat combined Axis I and Axis II conditions.

As will be noted in the specific treatment guidelines for the different anxiety disorders, combined conditions must be treated either before or concurrently with the anxiety disorder. Since personality pathology is present in 50 percent of panic/agoraphobic patients and interferes with both pharmacological and behavioral therapy interventions, focal psychotherapeutic intervention of the personality disorder is essential (Cowley & Roy-Byrne, 1988). Specific interventions are described in Chapter 13 of this book.

4. Enhance compliance by involving significant others in the treatment process.

There is considerable evidence that the spouses, parents, and friends of anxiety disorder patients can facilitate or hinder treatment outcomes. For instance, a husband may have considerable investment in the continuation of his wife's symptoms (Barlow & Waddell, 1985). Or, the marriage may be a mutually reinforcing system in which the agoraphobic individual is kept in a dependent stance by a spouse in order to cover up the latter's dependence and anger. Therein, the symptom bearer finds a symbolic means of communicating with and controlling the other. Such is the case for the wife whose symptoms leave her housebound and force the husband to postpone a business trip to take care of her.

At least three treatment options are available for involving significant others in combined treatment. The first is conjoint marital or couples therapy in which the spouse or significant other meets with the clinician and patient. Zitrin, Klein, and Woerner (1978) report that marital therapy combined with medication is extremely effective. Second, if the spouse is unwilling or unable to be involved in conjoint couples sessions, the patient can be treated individually with behavioral interventions in which the other spouse serves as the at-home coach or co therapist for the behavioral exposure training. Glick, Clarkin, and Goldsmith (1993) indicated that this approach was superior to the treatment condition where the spouse was not involved. Finally, Barlow and Waddell (1985) report a session-by-session account of time-limited group intervention involving five couples in which one spouse was agoraphobic.

5. Incorporate psychoeducation in treatment process.
Psychoeducation with anxiety disorders can involve patient and family education courses, self-help groups, and bibliotherapy. Bisbee's manual (1991) *Educating Patients and Families About Mental Illness: A Practical Guide* has excellent teaching modules for patient and family teaching. The OC Foundation and the Phobia Society of America offer local chapter and support groups. There are several excellent trade books, booklets, and pamphlets to educate patients and their families about the anxiety disorders and treatment options. The booklets *Obsessive Compulsive Disorder: A Guide* and *Panic Disorder and Agoraphobia: A Guide* by Greist and Jefferson (1992) are highly recommended as adjuncts to the office-based psychiatrist's treatment. Both booklets provide simple, concise, step-by-step exposure protocols for guiding the patients through sessions of exposure training. The booklets also provide the patient with a rationale for combined treatment, information on medication and behavior therapy, and answers to commonly asked questions.

6. Anticipate and initiate prevention procedure.
Relapse prevention is an intervention strategy that prepares the pa-

tient in advance to cope with the inevitable slips or relapses that occur during the course of a change program. Relapse or recurrence of symptoms is most likely to occur among patients taking only medication, when the medication is discontinued. Most relapses occur within the first two months after TCA discontinuation. Even for patients who improve, most continue to suffer some residual symptoms. Those with phobic avoidant behavior may continue to be symptomatic as long as their fear of anxiety symptoms and propensity to avoid treatment are incompletely treated. It is for that reason that combined treatment involving cognitive-behavioral interventions plus medication is advocated. Typically, both treatments begin concurrently and medication is tapered later while the cognitive-behavioral continues (Pollack & Otto, 1994).

Cognitive-behavioral interventions have also been utilized as the only treatment modality. With some patients no medication is needed. However, the occasional recurrence of anxiety symptoms is not uncommon in patients who have successfully completed behavioral treatment. Relapse prevention prepares the patient for dealing with stressful situations and triggers, as well as with relapses, if and when they occur. In the treatment of the anxiety disorders, relapse prevention starts the first time the clinician and patient discuss the importance of approaching rather than avoiding the feared object or situation (Butler, 1989).

The following sections briefly describe guidelines and combined treatment of five anxiety disorders: panic and agoraphobia; obsessive compulsive disorder; generalized anxiety disorder; social phobia; and simple phobia.

PANIC AND AGORAPHOBIA

There is extensive literature on the combined treatment of both panic and agoraphobic disorders. The results are quite instructive. Exposure-based treatment has been shown to be as effective as medication for the treatment of both disorders. But while relapse is common when medication is discontinued, the effects of exposure endure after formal treatment is completed. Thus, combining both modalities initially is considered the treatment of choice for most patients. The recommendation is for both treatments to be started simultaneously, with medication to be weaned when symptoms begin to remit, while continuing exposure (Mavissakalian, 1993).

The use of benzodiazepines has been questioned in combined treatment, largely because they appear to interfere with exposure training and other behavioral therapy interventions (Mavissakalian, 1993). Greist (1992b) speculates this is due to state-dependent learning, i.e., what patients learn while taking the benzodiazepine is lost when they stop taking it. Shear (1991) provides recommendations for tailoring treatment with patients who have poor medication tolerance and compliance. Greist and Jefferson's patient booklet on panic and agoraphobia (1992) is an excellent adjunct to office-based combined treatment. Self-help materials may significantly reduce symptoms and serve as a powerful treatment adjunct (Otto, Gould, & Pollack, 1994).

Even among patients who show improvement, many continue to suffer some residual symptoms. Often, the reasons include poor compliance, an untreated comorbid psychiatric or medical condition, improper medication strategy–insufficient dose, frequency, or duration, or negative attitude toward medication (Pollack & Otto, 1994). Thus, a complete diagnostic is needed.

GUIDELINES FOR PANIC AND/OR AGORAPHOBIA

1. **A thorough diagnostic evaluation is essential.**
   Before treatment can begin, stimulants (nicotine, caffeine, and other xanthene) must be reduced or stopped. Alcohol and substance abuse or dependence must first be treated before initiating any of the following guidelines.
2. **Medication (antidepressant or benzodiazepine) is typically the initial treatment.**
   That is, unless the patient presents with any of the following: (a) refusal to take, failure to respond, or poor tolerance of the medication; (b) reappearance of symptoms after medication is stopped; or (c) residual symptoms remain while at therapeutic levels. If any one or all are present, add behavioral interventions and/or psychotherapy. A variety of pharmacologic strategies for those refractory to a single medication should be tried. If the initial antidepressant is a tricyclic or SSRI and is not effective, an adequate trial of an MAOI should be considered. Switching to another class of

antidepressants or an augmentation strategy, such as adding valproic acid, lithium, or busprone, may also be tried (Pollack & Otto, 1994).

3. **The treatment of choice for most patients will be combined treatment: Antidepressant plus exposure therapy.**
   Add exposure therapy after medication is begun. When symptom relief is achieved, begin weaning and eventually discontinue medication while continuing exposure.
4. **For individuals in combined treatment with poor medication tolerance, various options exist.**
   They are: identify the cognitive and interpersonal roots of medication-triggered anxiety; educate the patient and correct misinformation about the meaning and consequences of panic episodes and medication; delay beginning medication while patients convince themselves of the acceptability of the medication trial; and controlled breathing training may be useful for patients experiencing jitteriness response to tricyclics.
5. **Benzodiazepines and other drugs that affect state-dependent learning (barbiturates, antihistamines, hydroxyzine, meprobamate) tend to interfere with exposure training and should be avoided.**
   Greist and Jefferson (1992) offer this explanation for loss of treatment effect and recurrence of symptoms.
6. **For patients only partially responsive to combined treatment, the presence of treatment antagonistic personality factor or personality disorder must be identified.**
   Patients with comorbid personality disorders, especially dependent, histrionic, and avoidant, require focal psychotherapy in addition to medication and exposure training. This psychotherapy should be targeted at changing ingrained avoidance patterns of thinking and behavior.
7. **Noncompliance arises for several reasons.**
   First, patients who remain intensely fearful tend to balk when exposure training is prescribed. They primarily need medication alone, with a graduated exposure schedule. Second, they may perceive treatment as ineffective or not credible. Exploring their treatment expectations and fantasies about their illness is necessary. Third, a lack of social support can minimize motivation as well as readiness to relinquish their pattern of avoidance. Fourth, concurrent depression can also reduce motivation for compliance with psychosocial interventions (Craske & Waikar, 1994).

8. **Group therapy can be particularly valuable not only in the treatment of panic and agoraphobic symptoms, but also in enhancing compliance and adherence.**
   Cognitive-behavioral groups have been shown to be effective with panic and agoraphobia, particularly techniques such as group *in vivo* exposure and relearning (Brook, 1993). Barlow and Waddell (1985) describe a 10-session treatment protocol for couples therapy for agoraphobia.
9. **Marital therapy or the addition of a significant other as a co-therapist in behavioral component may be indicated.**
   When the significant other is hostile, critical, and unsupportive, or has some investment in the patient's symptom picture, involving that significant other in treatment may be necessary. On the other hand, when these negative features are not present, the agoraphobic patient may be successfully treated individually with behavioral interventions (Glick, Clarkin, & Goldsmith, 1993).
10. **Relapse prevention is a critical issue in the treatment of the anxiety disorders, especially when medication has been the sole treatment.**
    For this reason, combined treatment involving both a cognitive-behavioral approach and medication, as well as a relapse prevention plan, is necessary. The patient should be helped to develop and write such a plan. Booster sessions may also be helpful. When indicated, they can be scheduled at intervals of two, four, and eight months after treatment is terminated.

OBSESSIVE COMPULSIVE DISORDER

Combined treatment–behavior therapy plus anafranil or a serotonergic uptake inhibitor–is the treatment of choice for most patients (Mavissakalian, 1993; Greist, 1992a; Jenike, 1991). Above one-half of patients show marked response with behavioral therapy alone, and half show marked improvement with anafranil, with one-third being nearly symptom-free (Mavissakalian et al., 1990). The antiobsessional effect of medication appears to be independent of their antidepressant effect and is postulated to be mediated through serotonergic mechanism.

Neither cognitive nor dynamic therapy has proved effective with OCD (Greist & Jefferson, 1992). Behavior therapy consists of exposure plus response prevention. In response prevention, patients are taught to prevent themselves from engaging in the ritualistic behavior. Psychiatrists can provide such treatment from their offices and need refer only patients who fail to respond to a behavior therapist with expertise in OCD, while continuing to assure adequate pharmacological intervention. Greist (1992a) reports that substantial improvement can take place with limited clinician involvement. A total of 3 1/2 hours of office-based treatment spread over 17 weeks was needed, on the average, to effect this improvement. During these sessions the clinician assisted patients to design and implement their own homework-based exposure and response prevention program. The patients were initially prescribed three hours a day of graduated exposure and response prevention tasks at home. As symptoms remitted, less time per day would be prescribed. Jenike (1991) insists that substance abuse and dependence must be treated before one attempts to treat OCD. He provides a detailed combined treatment protocol for the patient with severe personality disorder pathology, especially schizotypal personality disorder. The interested reader is referred to this source (Jenike, 1991).

GUIDELINES FOR OBSESSIVE COMPULSIVE DISORDER

1. **A complete diagnostic evaluation is essential.**
   It is necessary because manic, psychotic, cognitively impaired, and severely personality-disordered patients require special treatment strategies and guidelines beyond those listed below. Alcohol and other substance abuse and dependence must be treated before the OCD treatment can be initiated.
2. **If the patient is severely depressed, is purely obsessional, is taking CNS depressing medication, or refuses behavioral interventions, begin psychopharmacology with anafranil or a serotonergic uptake inhibitor.**
   Medication is usually required for most OCD patients at some point in treatment, particularly when the aforementioned indications are present.
3. **If rituals are present, or the patient has a drug allergy or is reluctant to begin a medication trial, begin with office-based behavior therapy.**
   This would include instruction on behavioral exposure training and response prevention training, supplemented with between-ses-

sion homework assignments (initially three hrs/day). Providing the patient with a copy of *Obsessive Compulsive Disorder: A Guide* (Greist, 1992b) is recommended.

4. **For most patients, a combination of behavior therapy (exposure and response prevention) with a serotonergic uptake inhibitor is the treatment of choice, with both treatments starting simultaneously.**
   Research consistently shows the value of this particular treatment combination (Mavissakalian, 1993).
5. **Provide focal psychotherapy for an Axis II disorder and/or to increase compliance treatability.**
   As previously indicated, personality pathology can negatively impact efforts to treat Axis I symptomatology.
6. **If there is an unsatisfactory response, consider the following: (a) consultation with or referral to a behavior therapist with OCD expertise; (b) reevaluation of dosage, duration, and medication compliance.**
   Consider utilizing an augmentation strategy that further enhances serotonergic activity or decrease dopaminergic, particularly when a concomitant schizotypal personality disorder or tic disorder is present; or switch to another serotonergic agent.
7. **If treatment fails, rediagnose and consider referral for psychosurgery for very severe intractable conditions.**
   Often, another diagnostic evaluation reveals the unexpected: an undetected or untreated substance disorder, the presence of schizotypal personality disorder, a space-occupying lesion, etc. If no such diagnosis can be made, and all other medication trials, including augmentation, have failed, a neurosurgical consult can be made.
8. **Relapse prevention is an important part of the treatment plan in OCD.**
   The patient should be helped to develop and write a personalized relapse prevention plan. This plan should specify high-risk circumstances and triggers, as well as a plan for anticipating and dealing with them. Adverse life events and depression are often associated with the reemergence of OCD symptoms. Since exposure and response prevention are primary intervention strategies, the patient must be coached in applying them in times of relapse. Booster sessions may be necessary to reestablish symptom remis-

sion. The availability of these sessions should be made known and the patient should be encouraged to schedule them as needed.

GENERALIZED ANXIETY DISORDER (GAD)

Treatment of GAD needs to address not only symptomatology, but also underlying psychological, behavioral, and biological determinants. Beaudry (1991) suggests that treatment needs to be tailored based on age, severity and chronicity, social content, and the presence of personality disorders. When anxiety is mild, Beaudry suggests beginning with psychotherapy. He notes that supportive psychotherapy is as effective as intensive psychotherapy or behavior therapy. With more severe anxiety, he suggests the use of medication, with combined treatment recommended for the most severe.

Mavissakalian (1993) reports that GAD responds equally well to benzodiazepines, antidepressants, and cognitive-behavioral treatments, especially exposure. Usually medication use is short-term. If long-term, continuation medication is anticipated, antidepressants are favored over traditional benzodiazepines. He notes that cognitive restructuring has been successful in identifying subtle and ingrained self-perpetuating escape-avoidance mechanisms. Combined treatment may be particularly useful in severe cases of generalized anxiety (Beaudry, 1991).

GUIDELINES FOR GENERALIZED ANXIETY DISORDER

1. **A complete functional psychiatric evaluation is a prerequisite for tailoring treatment based on the patient's perpetuants, pattern, and prognostic factors.**
   Alcohol and/or substance abuse or dependence must be treated prior to treatment of GAD.
2. **Treatment modality depends on the severity of the anxiety.**
   For mild cases, psychotherapy may be sufficient. For moderate anxiety, medication or cognitive behavior therapy with exposure training is indicated.
3. **Combined treatment is probably indicated for severe anxiety.**

In treatment-resistant cases, an undiagnosed or untreated substance or personality disorder is probably present. Appropriate focal psychotherapeutic interventions should be added to the combined treatment.

4. **Strategies for preventing relapse and maintaining gains should be incorporated throughout treatment and emphasized as termination draws near.**
   If the patient had been on medication, it usually will be weaned and discontinued by this time. The patient should be helped to write an individualized relapse prevention plan that includes high-risk circumstances and triggers along with the specific preventive measures, including desensitization strategies. Toward the end of treatment, the patient's expectations of future worries about anxiety episodes should be frankly discussed. Roleplaying can be utilized to prepare for such newly encountered situations. One or two booster sessions can be scheduled at four and eight week intervals to review progress as well as maintenance and relapse issues.

SOCIAL PHOBIAS

Recent research and DSM-IV criteria support the clinical observation that social phobia is not a unified diagnosis. There appears to be a generalized form of social phobia that overlaps considerably with avoidant personality disorder (Uhde & Tancer, 1991). Fortunately, this generalized form is quite responsive to MAOIs and serotonergic agents, whereas beta blockers are effective with focal social phobia (Liebowitz et al., 1991). There has been an increasing amount of research literature on the combined treatment of social phobia that suggests that social phobia is highly responsive to a variety of therapeutic modalities.

Alprazolam, phenelzine, and cognitive behavioral intervention incorporating exposure have been shown to be equally effective in a placebo-controlled study (Gelernter et al., 1991). Preliminary results comparing phenelzine and exposure showed that both modalities have equal efficacy, with approximately 80 percent response rates (Heimberg & Liebowitz, 1992). Uhde and Tancer (1991) note that some patients respond better to combined treatment, and thus recommend it when there is only partial response with either modality.

Concurrent psychopathology complicates the treatment of social phobia. Common comorbid conditions are panic/agoraphobia, depression, obsessive compulsive disorder, alcohol dependence, and personality disorders. Rosenbaum and Pollack (1994) offer pharmacological strategies for these five conditions.

GUIDELINES FOR SOCIAL PHOBIAS

1. **A complete functional psychiatric evaluation is needed to diagnose concurrent alcohol and substance abuse or dependence.** These must be treated before one initiates treatment of the phobia. Detoxification is necessary to establish the patient's baseline functioning and to diagnose a treatable Axis I disorder.
2. **Begin treatment with either medication or cognitive behavioral therapy, depending on patient preference and/or clinician's expertise.**
   Assuming the symptom presentation is mild to moderate, either modality can be effective.
3. **When treatment outcomes are limited, consider combined treatment.**
   As with other anxiety disorders, combined treatment is particularly useful with moderately severe to severe presentations.
4. **Relapse prevention is more an issue with the generalized rather than with the focal form of social phobia.**
   Whereas brief targeted interventions may be sufficient for the focal form, the generalized form may require longer-term treatment, particularly for individuals with dependent or avoidant personality structures. Developing an individualized relapse prevention plan and booster sessions are necessary. Scheduling booster sessions at monthly intervals for four months and then spaced two months apart for a further eight months may be indicated (Mattick & Andrews, 1994).

SIMPLE PHOBIAS

Simple phobia rarely results in marked impairment and, thus, individuals with this disorder rarely seek treatment. However, sufficient impairment or distress may lead to treatment. Of all the anxiety disorders, simple phobias are exquisitely responsive to exposure therapy, often remitting entirely in a single therapy session (Ost, 1989). The general psychiatrist might attempt this treatment or refer to a behavior therapist with expertise in simple phobias. Because of the circumscribed, situation-specific nature of the symptom (i.e., fear of spiders, sight of blood, or heights) medications are not usually indicated (Mavissakalian, 1993). However, Mavissakalian (1993) notes that it may be clinically useful to enable patients to engage in an "unavoidable" situation on a given occasion.

GUIDELINES FOR SIMPLE PHOBIAS

1. **A complete functional psychiatric evaluation is essential.** It is needed to rule out that the phobic avoidance is not associated with schizophrenia, post-traumatic stress disorder, obsessive compulsive disorder, or a medical condition.
2. **Employ exposure therapy or refer patient to a behavior therapist with expertise in simple phobias.** Clark (1989) describes exposure protocol that most clinicians with little or no behavior therapy can easily master. Behavior therapists who specialize in simple phobia treatment can often effect a cure in a single session.
3. **Medications are contraindicated in simple phobias.** However, a limited course of benzodiazepine might be prescribed to enable the phobic patient to engage in an otherwise "unavoidable" situation.
4. **Fear levels may increase some time after treatment.** Thus, patients should be instructed to anticipate and be prepared for it. They should also be instructed not to give in to the impulse to avoid or escape the fear, but to face it as they had learned. An individualized relapse plan should be developed prior to termination. Although there is less likelihood that patients with simple phobia will need booster sessions, that option should be made known to the patient.

PATIENT AND FAMILY RESOURCES

Reading Materials

- *Anxiety and Its Treatment: Help Is Available* by John Greist, M.D., James Jefferson, M.D., and Isaac Marks, M.D., American Psychiatric Press and Warner Books, 1986.
- *Coping with Panic* by G. A. Clum, Brooks/Cole Publishing, 1990.
- *Peace from Nervous Suffering* by Claire Weeks, M.D., Bantam Books, 1978.
- *The Anxiety Disease* by David Sheehan, M.D., Bantam Books, 1983.
- *Obsessive Compulsive Disorder: A Guide* by John Greist, M.D. Information Centers, Dean Foundation, 8000 Excelsior Drive, Madison, WI 53717 (608) 836-8079, 1992.
- *Panic Disorder and Agoraphobia: A Guide* by John Greist, M.D. and James Jefferson, M.D., Information Centers, Dean Foundation, 8999 Excelsior Drive, Madison, WI 53717 (608)836-8079, 1992.
- *When One Is Not Enough: Help for Obsessive Compulsives* by Gail Stehelee, Ph.D. and Kay White, New Harbinger Publications, 1990.
- *The Boy Who Couldn't Stop Washing: The Experience and Treatment of Obsessive Compulsive Disorders* by Judith Rapoport, M.D., Dutton, 1989.

Self-Help Groups and Organizations

Phobia Society of America publishes a national directory of treatment centers and providers, sponsors an annual conference, provides training materials, promotes public education, and has local chapters and support groups. The Society can be reached at 133 Rollins Avenue, Suite 4B, Rockville, MD 20852; (301) 331-9350.

OC Foundation, Inc. is a national organization devoted to education, research, and service to families and professionals to assist those with OCD. The foundation can be reached at P.O. Box 9573, New Haven, CT 06535; (203) 772-0565.

10

Bipolar Disorder

The striking success of lithium's calming effect on bipolar disorder and published case reports of lithium producing significant improvement were sometimes misconstrued as reports of cure and gave rise to an enduring treatment mythology. The most frequently repeated myth is that lithium alone is effective therapy for all but 30 percent of bipolar patients (Sachs et al., 1994). Although biological factors predominate in the etiology and course of bipolar disorder, the primary manifestations of the disorder are psychological and behavioral, with profound changes in personality, mood, perception, attitude, and cognition.

A biopsychosocial model of bipolar disorder has been proposed (Post, Rubinow & Ballenger, 1986; Post, 1992) based on the "kindling hypothesis." In short, this model suggests that repeated emotional stressors in a vulnerable individual sensitize and cause recurrent affective episodes. Furthermore, psychological intervention occurs early in the course of the illness, the vulnerability can be modified. However, if no effective intervention occurs, the disorder can be self-generating apart from apparent stressors. In short, psychosocial intervention along with medications can "immunize" the patient against subsequent recurrence.

Not surprisingly, psychosocial treatment can be of inestimable value to bipolar patients (Jamison, 1991). This chapter describes specific treatment strategies and guidelines for the bipolar disorder. It will challenge clinicians probably more than any other chapter in this section because it addresses a number of myths and sacred cows in the clinical lore surrounding treatment of a psychiatric disorder.

COMBINING TREATMENT MODALITIES IN BIPOLAR DISORDER

While antimanic agents free most patients from the severe disruptions of manic and depressive episodes, psychotherapy helps patients come to terms with the repercussions of past episodes and comprehend the practical and existential implications of having bipolar disorder. Although not all patients require psychotherapy, most can benefit from one of its modalities: individual, family, or group.

1. Most bipolar patients should be offered combined individual and medication treatment.

This combined treatment is the most common, whether in specialized "lithium clinics" or in general psychiatric practice (Schou, 1991). Patients who engage in a psychotherapeutic process are more likely to comply with medication regimens, are less likely to deny their illness, suffer less trauma from having bipolar disorder, and show improved social and occupational functioning. Furthermore, relapse and recurrence are considerably reduced with this form of combined treatment (Fuerst, 1994).

Nevertheless, prescribing clinicians seem to be rather ambivalent about the role of psychotherapy and their own psychotherapeutic role in the treatment of bipolar disorder. One study, revealed that patients were twice as likely as clinicians to believe that psychotherapy aided medication compliance (Jamison, 1991). Limited clinical knowledge and experience with combined treatment, as well as countertransferences such as: "No one should feel this good, I'm glad the patient crashed," further reinforce the myth that lithium–or another antimanic–alone cures.

Psychotherapeutic support is essential when only medication-monitoring sessions are possible. The clinician can establish an emotionally supportive atmosphere, be cognizant of and focus on general issues related to bipolar illness–specifically dependency, loss, and need for medication, and encourage patients to express their concerns. Providing such a therapeutic relationship increases the likelihood of medication compliance and sets the stage for formal psychotherapy should it be indicated.

Formal individual psychotherapy is indicated in the following situations: those unwilling to take medication in the prescribed manner, those who are suicidal, those in whom an Axis II personality disorder is prominent, and those for whom issues of dependency and symbolic loss are particularly problematic (Goodwin & Jamison, 1990; Jamison, 1991; Jamison & Goodwin, 1983).

Issues of dependency and counterdependency, poor self-esteem, problems of intimacy, medication noncompliance, and denial of their illness are major issues in psychotherapy of bipolar patients. There are different clinical formulations of the diagnosis of the bipolar disorder. While the analyst attributes the cause of the disorder and associated personality deficits to the early family environment, Jamison and Goodwin (1983) believe that the traumatic experience of the disorder itself and nature of treatment result in the losses that dominate the patient's life. Accordingly, they advocate focusing treatment on losses: realistic, symbolic, and unrealistic losses; fears of recurrence; and denial of illness. Realistic losses include decreased energy level, loss of euphoric states, increased need for sleep, decreased sexuality, and possible decreases in productivity. Symbolic losses include loss of perceived omnipotence and independence. Unrealistic losses include circumstances where the antimanic agent and psychotherapy come to symbolize the patient's personal failure. Thus, the antimanic becomes a psychological "whipping boy" representing other failures predating the onset of the bipolar illness. A major task of treatment is to help the patient understand and mourn these losses.

Kahn (1990) offers a synthesis of Jamison and Goodwin's problem-solving approach with the psychoanalytic approach. Kahn would focus individual psychotherapy on seven areas: realistic losses; symbolic losses; concerns about genetic transmission; effects on family, spouse, and others; fears of recurrence; problems in learning to discriminate normal from abnormal moods; and interrupted developmental tasks, particularly if the disorder began during adolescence.

2. When appropriate, incorporate family therapy with medication management.

There are at least three indications for combined family and medication treatment: to increase medication compliance; to reduce relapse; and to increase social support, especially for high-risk patients. Family stress, particularly expressed emotion and a rejecting attitude, are predictors of relapse. High levels of family rejection together with previous hospitalizations and medication noncompliance have been shown to predict rehospitalization within 18 months (Glick, Clarkin & Goldsmith, 1993). Miklowitz has developed a behavioral family management intervention for bipolar patients which is described under Guideline #3 below (Fuerst, 1994). Davenport et al. (1977) describe the use of couples therapy in the long-term treatment of married bipolar patients on medication.

3. Consider group therapy as an adjunct to antimanic medication when indicated.

Indications for combined group therapy include: medication noncompliance; relapse prevention; social support–in the absence of a supportive family; and to increase social skills and functioning. Most of the studies on combined group and medication treatment involve homogeneous groups, that is, all patients carried the diagnosis of bipolar disorder. Kanas (1993) has reviewed four such studies. Common goals in these groups were: sharing information about the illness; learning strategies for coping with it; and improving interpersonal relationships. To achieve these goals, treatment interventions included education, support, and facilitation of group discussions.

4. For the lithium-resistant bipolar patient, utilize a multimodal approach.

The great majority of bipolar patients respond to some form of combined treatment. It has been estimated that only 5–10 percent of bipolars are truly treatment resistant. According to Frederick Goodwin, M.D. (Zoler, 1994), two factors account for lithium resistance: substance abuse and the increased use of tricyclic antidepressants with bipolar patients. About 60 percent of bipolar patients have a substance abuse history and must be detoxed before treatment for the bipolar illness is started. Because of the increased incidence of inducing rapid cycling, tricyclics should not be routinely prescribed. Instead, an MAOI or serotonergic agent might be considered. Or, if a tricyclic must be used–as with severe depression–it should be tapered as soon as remission occurs.

The utilization of lithium augmentation is recommended. Valproate, carbomezaprine, MAOI, thyroxin, or a calcium channel blocker like verapamil are suggested. Nonmedication modalities such as sleep deprivation and high-density light therapy are also recommended by Goodwin. Such a multimodal approach to supplement apparent lithium resistance should be done in a sequential fashion, adding each modality slowly and in a logical way (Zoler, 1994).

ENHANCING MEDICATION COMPLIANCE AND TREATMENT ADHERENCE WITH BIPOLAR PATIENTS

Noncompliance with antimanic agents is costly not only to patients and their families but to society as well. Patients who fail to comply with medication have a rather predictable profile, and they cite medication side effects and numerous psychological factors as the reasons for their noncompliance. A number of strategies to enhance compliance are provided.

1. Evaluate each patient for risk factors of noncompliance.

Patients who are at high risk for medication noncompliance are likely to have some or many factors of this profile: They are likely to be in the first year of antimanic treatment; they tend to have a prior history of medication noncompliance; they tend to be younger; they are more likely to be male; they have a history of grandiose, euphoric manias, rather than the bipolar type II presentation; they have elevated mood and fewer episodes; and they complain of "missing highs" when they are in remission of symptoms (Goodwin & Jamison, 1990).

2. Evaluate the patient's explanatory model as well as countertransference.

Clinical experience suggests that "missing highs" is the most ominous risk factor. Accordingly, the clinician would do well to elicit the patient's explanatory model, including what bipolar illness and its symptoms represent for him or her. Since mania or hypomania associated with bipolar is, for all practical purposes, an endogenous stimulant that can be quite addicting, the "high" is preferred to the "blahs" associated with medications. Noncompliance is the patient's strategy to induce mania not just when depressed but when faced with problematic decisions and life events. Since the negative consequences accrue only later, the patient may not easily comprehend how the costs of noncompliance outweigh the benefits.

Similarly, for the patient who has already had a trial of an antimanic, the learned association between the use of the antimanic and the subsequent normothymic or dysphoric state may come to symbolize a loss of innocence from prepsychotic to postpsychotic consciousness. Thus, medication noncompliance can represent an attempt to recapture an earlier prepsychotic existence, one not yet despoiled by mania or depression (Jamison & Goodwin, 1983).

Transference and countertransference can complicate treatment and may trigger noncompliance. For this reason, the clinician must carefully monitor and deal with both. In the manic phase, patients try to impress and manipulate or reject the clinician in an attempt to enhance self-esteem. Later, transference shifts to dependency in an effort to avoid further illness and suffering. This shift from manipulation or rejection to open dependency provides the clinician considerable therapeutic leverage. The main countertransference issues in bipolar patients are excessive anger or excessive fear. Urges to punish the patient are evidenced in many ways, including under- or overmedicating patients, which could result in noncompliance. Kahn (1990) further discusses these and other transference and countertransference issues.

3. Incorporate strategies for maximizing medication compliance in the treatment plan and process.

Goodwin and Jamison (1990) summarize six guidelines for maximizing compliance. They include: (1) monitoring compliance with regular inquiries about medication use, effects and side effects, as well as regular serum levels; (2) monitoring side effects and treating them aggressively; (3) education, particularly about prodromal signs and persistent symptoms; (4) effecting a reasonable dosing schedule and providing written instructions, as well as involving family members in administering medications, if appropriate; (5) adjunctive psychotherapy, and (6) self-help groups.

Cochran (1984) describes an individual psychotherapeutic format for enhancing compliance that is noteworthy. A clinician meets for six sessions of one hour each and follows a structured cognitive-behavioral outline. Topics include eliciting patients' beliefs about their illness and the medication, identifying and monitoring negative thoughts about medication, coping skills, and problem solving regarding medication issues. Not surprisingly, encouraging patients to express their beliefs and feelings about medication and then anticipating possible noncompliance issues not only increase commitment to treatment, but also prevent noncompliance.

INCORPORATE PSYCHOEDUCATION INTO THE TREATMENT OF THE BIPOLAR PATIENT

There are probably more forms of psychoeducation that are readily available to bipolar patients than there are for most other psychiatric disorders, particularly in the area of patient education and bibliotherapy. Other forms of psychoeducation include family education and intervention, and support groups.

1. Make patient education and bibliotherapy available to bipolar patient.

There are three booklets written by the staff of the nationwide Lithium Information Center that clinicians would do well to make available to their bipolar patients and their families. The titles of these books are listed below in the section entitled "Patient Resources." These booklets are informative as well as accurately representing the cutting edge of treatment for the bipolar disorder. The booklet includes a form for recording serum levels (lithium, carbamezapine, valproate) and a list of suggested technical and nontechnical readings. Since bipolar patients and their families tend to have higher levels of educational attainment, they are often quite interested and willing to learn more about their illness and its treatment. In addition, there are a number of autobiographies of recovery by bipolar patients. Patty Duke Astin, the actress, is a spokesperson for the NIMH on bipolar disorder and her book *A Brilliant Madness: Living with Manic Depressive Illness* (1992) has been well received by bipolar patients and their families. Some of these are listed in the "Patient Resources" section.

2. Incorporate family education and management when possible.

Bisbee's *Educating Patients and Families About Mental Illness* (1991) has a teaching module on bipolar disorder and its treatment with copy-ready material for overhead transparencies and handouts. This material can easily be incorporated into clinical practice. Miklowitz (Fuerst, 1994) has designed a behavioral family-management intervention for lower-functioning bipolar patients and their families. Used in conjunction with medication, this 21-session program is held in the patient's home over a period of nine months. After a functional assessment, the family is educated about bipolar disorder and its treatment, and then taught to improve family communication and problem solving. Results of the pilot study show increased compliance and reduced relapse.

3. Encourage patient involvement in community support groups.

Perhaps the oldest and most widely known support groups geared toward bipolar patients' needs are those sponsored by the National Depressive and Manic Depressive Association (NDMDA). The NDMDA has programs and materials directed to patients and their families. In addition to a network of local chapters throughout North America, the association sponsors an annual national convention, distributes audio and video programs, and publishes a national newsletter. The heart of NDMDA, however, lies in the scheduled community meetings, which consist of input from professionals in the community, in addition to a traditional support group function.

PREVENT RELAPSE AND RECURRENCE AMONG BIPOLAR PATIENTS

Relapse rates in bipolar disorders are estimated to be approximately 40 percent and are usually attributed to medication noncompliance (Kahn, 1990). Schou (1991) indicates that the treatment context is correlated with relapse and treatment dropout. Schou contends that where treatment is provided in a lithium or mood disorders clinic the dropout rate is 10 percent per year, while in other settings the dropout rate may be 50 percent within the first six months and increases to 90 percent in five years. The advantage of a specialty clinic is that clinicians have specialty training, can provide a consistent treatment environment, can select appropriate patients for treatment, and thus can more effectively motivate them to remain in treatment. The literature on relapse in bipolar disorder is rather sparse and focused largely on medication use (Goodwin & Jamison, 1990). For example, Schou's (1991) article on relapse prevention lists 14 guidelines, of which 12 are directly focused on medication and side effects! Nevertheless, Post's "kindling model" (1986) suggests that relapse and recurrence can be attenuated.

1. Develop a relapse prevention plan for each bipolar patient.

Post, Rubinow & Ballenger (1986) suggest that an important task of psychotherapy–or of other psychosocial interventions–is to develop a relapse plan. This would include a hierarchy of external events and cognition that are particularly prone to trigger dysphoria or hypomanic feeling. Since Post believes that bipolar disorder involves behavioral hypersensitivity which primes electrophysiological kindling, he recommends the focus of treatment be on "working through and systematic desensitization" (Post, Rubinow & Ballenger, 1986, p. 198).

PATIENT RESOURCES

Booklets

Available from the Lithium Information Center, Dean Foundation, 3000 Excelsior Drive, Suite 203, Madison, WI 53719–1914:

- *Lithium and Manic Depression: A Guide* (1992), by John Bohn, M.D., and James Jefferson, M.D. Madison, WI: Dean Foundation (30 pp).
- *Valproate and Manic Depression: A Guide* (1993) by James Jefferson, M.D., and John Greist, M.D. Madison, WI: Dean Foundation (30 pp).
- *Carbamezapine and Manic Depression: A Guide* (1990) by Janet Medenwald, M.D., John Greist, M.D., and James Jefferson, M.D. Madison, WI: Dean Foundation (30 pp).

Nontechnical Books

- *From Sad to Glad* (1987), by Nathan S. Kline, M.D. New York: Ballantine.
- *Moodswing* (1989), by Ronald L. Fieve, M.D. New York: Morrow.

Autobiographical Material in Bipolar Disorders

- *Call Me Anna: The Autobiography of Patty Duke* (1992), by Patty Duke. New York: Bantam.
- *A Brilliant Madness: Living with Manic-Depressive Illness* (1992), by Patty Duke. New York: Bantam.
- *Darkness Visible: A Memoir of Madness* (1990), by William Styron. New York: Random House.

Support Group

The National Depressive and Manic Depressive Association (NDMDA) has local chapters of support groups in most major U.S. and Canadian cities. Contact NDMDA at Merchandise Mart, Box 3395, Chicago, IL 60654, for information on local chapters or resource material.

11

Depression

The widely known NIMH Treatment of Depression Collaborative Research Program (Elkin et al., 1989) involved two treatment conditions in which medication was combined with cognitive therapy or interpersonal therapy. This program indirectly effected a major shift in the way psychiatric treatment outcomes were researched and in the way psychiatric treatment was practiced. It significantly impacted clinical practice, even to the very vocabulary used by clinicians. Today, terms like "symptom-focused treatment," "time-limited therapy," "manual-based therapy," and, especially, "combined treatments" are part of the common currency of exchange among mental health professionals.

Post et al. (1986; 1992) described a biopsychosocial model for understanding the etiology of affective disorders based on behavioral sensitization and physiological kindling. A similar sensitization model has been posited for the etiology of anxiety disorder (see Chapter 9). In both sensitization models, desensitization is a therapeutic mechanism. This chapter describes specific therapeutic strategies and treatment guidelines for desensitizing, that is, effectively treating, the depressive disorders.

COMBINING TREATMENTS WITH DEPRESSED PATIENTS

This section describes specific treatment guidelines for various combinations of medication and psychotherapy modalities. The combined modalities are individual, group, marital, and family psychotherapy, and psychosocial interventions.

1. Individual intervention strategies that include medication should be offered to patients who meet specific indications.

Joyce (1992) lists five predictors for positive responses to antidepressants alone. They are: good premorbid personality; psychomotor retardation; an intermediate level of severity and endogeneity; no psychotic features; and the absence of "atypical" features, i.e., panic attacks or reversed vegetative symptoms. In their exhaustive evaluation of the research studies summarized in their monograph, Manning and Frances (1990) found that there was a U-shaped relationship between the use of combined treatment and the severity of depression. They contend that combined treatment should be offered to those in the middle: from moderate to moderately severe depression. For those with mild depression, psychotherapy is the initial treatment of choice, while for very severe depression, medication and hospitalization are usually required as the initial treatment of choice. Only after some recompensation is achieved can combined treatment be considered. Thus, combined treatment for major depression is the first-line treatment for patients midway between the extreme of mild and very severe.

While it would be nice to conclude that cognitive therapy or interpersonal psychotherapy medication is superior in all respects to either modality alone, controlled trials report a different conclusion (Murphy, Simons, Wetzel, et al., 1984; Hollon, DeRubeis, Evans, et al., 1992). Rather there is consistent evidence that medications appear to work more rapidly than most psychotherapies–cognitive therapy excluded–and may depend less on the provider's skill for their effect. Conversely, psychotherapy does more to enhance social functioning–especially interpersonal psychotherapy–and to provide broad enduring change than do medications alone (Hallon & Fawcett, 1995).

Manning and Frances (1990) report that cognitive therapy plus medication had an additive effect with regard to preventing relapse (Hollon et al., 1992). Some specific contraindications for time-limited course of cognitive therapy and medication were noted: organic brain syndrome, severe depression with hallucinations or delusions, and schizoaffective disorder. In addition social systems factors such as negative attitudes of family members and hopelessness regarding the patient's depression negatively impacted the combined cognitive therapy-medication treatment. Finally, cognitive therapy and medication are so compatible that either can be added readily after the other has begun without adversely affecting the treatment process (Rush & Hollon, 1991).

Interpersonal psychotherapy (Weisman & Klerman, 1991) plus medication also had an additive effect with regard to preventing relapse, and also decreased premature dropout from treatment. In addition, interpersonal therapy and medication increased acceptance of treatment and led to more rapid and pervasive symptom improvement than placebo, medication alone, or cognitive therapy. Finally, interpersonal psychotherapy seemed to be more effective with more severe presentations of depression than cognitive therapy.

2. When indicated, consider combining group therapy with medication.

Although Manning and Frances (1990) found only a marginal advantage to combining group therapy and medication as compared to each alone, Salvendy and Toffe (1991) found that combined treatment enabled 83 percent of patients to achieve positive treatment outcomes, as compared to 60 percent on medication only. They offer indications and contraindications for this form of combined treatment. Positive responders are individuals who most resemble this profile: (1) have had at least one good relationship prior to treatment; (2) have achieved a reasonable self-concept; (3) are capable of trusting others; (4) have few problems with control issues; (5) are capable of establishing rapport with the group therapist; (6) are willing to take risks; and (7) were capable of engaging and becoming integrated into the group at the time of referral. Nonresponders tended to include patients with prominent narcissistic and/or borderline features, or patients with hypochondriacal or significant somatoform presentations. Brook (1993) suggests that the type of group therapy offered should be consonant with the severity and chronicity of the depression. He favors homogeneous medication groups, supportive groups, or cognitive-behavior groups for more severe and chronic depressed patients, while interpersonal and psycho-dynamically oriented groups are considered more appropriate for less severe and less chronic patients.

3. When indicated, combine family therapy and medication with depressed patients.

When marital or family conflict appear to be the primary precipitant in episodes of clinical depression, marital or family therapy is probably indicated for treatment of interpersonal conflict. Such treatment would be directed at reducing the frequency of aversive communication, increasing the number of positive experiences between family members, and modifying distorted cognitive and perceptual responses to the behavior of the identified patient. Typically, in major depression, medication is begun first. Then, after florid symptoms have diminished, conjoint couples or family sessions are begun (Glick et al., 1993).

ENHANCING MEDICATION COMPLIANCE AND TREATMENT ADHERENCE WITH DEPRESSED PATIENTS

1. Evaluate depressed patient for risk factors of noncompliance.
The literature on medication compliance regarding patients is relatively sparse. Like other psychiatric disorders, noncompliance is relatively high, in the range of 40 percent. Rehm, LePage, and Bailey (1994) profile the high-risk patient for noncompliance and treatment dropout. The profile indicates that patients with lower level of formal education, lower income or socioeconomic status, and severe levels of depression are most likely to prematurely terminate therapy. However, similar patients with mild to moderate severity of depression are more likely to be noncompliant with medication.

2. Incorporate strategies to maximize medication compliance in the treatment plan and process.
The cognitive therapy of depression (Beck et al., 1979; Rush, 1988) typically incorporates strategies to enhance compliance with medication and adherence to treatment, particularly homework assignments and monitoring dysfunctional thoughts. The collaborative nature of treatment approaches like cognitive therapy naturally fosters compliance and adherence. See Chapter 6 for further guidelines on compliance and adherence.

Research by Frank et al. (1992) showed that medication compliance is not related to age, sex, type of depression, or initial or baseline severity of depression. Rather, compliance was significantly associated with the adequacy of prophylaxis and the involvement of the patient's significant other (Frank, Kupfer, Perel, et al., 1990). In other words, when medication levels were subtherapeutic or intermittent, noncompliance was likely. Mann (1986) contends that the critical factor in compliance with antidepressants is sensitivity to the patient's subjective response to medication. The more side effects that patients experience that are unheeded, the more likely they are to either stop medication entirely or titrate down their dosage without telling the prescribing clinician (Fawcett, 1995).

INCORPORATE PSYCHOEDUCATION INTO THE TREATMENT OF THE DEPRESSED PATIENT

A considerable number of psychoeducational interventions regarding depression have been developed. As with the treatment of other psychiatric disorders described in Part III of this book, psychoeducational interventions can "supercharge" treatment process and outcome. This section briefly describes three classes of psychoeducational intervention: bibliotherapy and patient educational materials, medication groups, and community support groups.

1. Make patient education and bibliotherapy available to depressed patients and their families.

Bibliotherapy has proven to be surprisingly effective in the amelioration of symptoms and, some would say, in the cure of depression (Hoberman & Lewisohn, 1990). Lewisohn and his colleagues (1978) have developed an intervention called the "Coping with Depression" course which consists of 12 two-hour sessions conducted over eight weeks in group sessions, or held twice a week during the first four weeks of treatment and once a week for the final four weeks. The course has a didactic format that permits more group interaction. It emphasizes the attainment of knowledge and skills rather than an intensive relationship with a clinician. A basic premise of the course is that depression results from a decrease of pleasant and increase of unpleasant experiences, and that treatment of depression requires that unpleasant experiences decrease, while pleasant experiences increase.

The content of the course has been adapted to a book format. The paperback, *Control Your Depression* (Lewisohn et al., 1978) essentially is a condensation of the course. Several studies cited by Hoberman and Lewisohn (1990) demonstrate that either participation in the course or use of the book produces improvement equivalent to other forms of individual or group therapy. By and large, persons with mild to moderate depression who haven't been taking a prescribed antidepressant are candidates for this form of psychoeducation. Hoberman and Lewisohn list five predictors of positive treatment response: (1) higher expectation of improvement; (2) greater perceived control over symptoms; (3) lack of concurrent psychotherapy or medication; (4) higher levels of perceived family support; and (5) younger age. The two most powerful predictors are expectation of improvement and perceived control over symptoms. The value of the book as bibliotherapy for more severely depressed patients already in combined treatment has also been demonstrated.

Bisbee's (1991) *Educating Patients and Families About Mental Illness: A Practical Guide* has excellent modules on depression and its treatment. This material lends itself to individual or class use with patient and/or family members. Materials are camera-ready for making overhead transparencies and handouts.

2. Refer patients with chronic, severe depression to homogeneous medication groups.

Homogeneous medication groups, that is, groups where all patients carry the diagnosis of a depressive disorder, have particular value for depressed patients who are lower functioning and/or have a chronic, recurring pattern of episodes. The emphasis in medication groups is on education, compliance, and socialization. The goals are to increase patients' knowledge about their illness and its treatment, to decrease the isolation of patients and increase social skills, to allow for the expression of feeling in a safe and nonjudgmental environment, and to provide group support (Brook, 1993). The methodology of such groups is supportive and educational. Concurrent individual sessions should be made available when necessary. See Chapter 7 for guidelines on the use of medication groups and for the use of concurrent individual sessions.

3. Encourage patient involvement in community support groups.

The National Depressive and Manic Depressive Association (NDMDA) has local chapters, educational resource materials, and newsletters. It sponsors community support groups in many metropolitan areas of the United States and Canada. Typically, support groups meet weekly. In some communities, one or two meetings a month have professionals scheduled to address specific treatment issues or new medications, followed by questions and answers, while the other meetings are devoted to a self-help, support-group format. Patients and their families have profited from involvement with NDMDA activities, particularly in the support groups.

PREVENT RELAPSE AND RECURRENCE AMONG DEPRESSED PATIENTS

Rates of relapse are exceptionally high among depressed patients. More than 50 percent experience relapse within three months after discontinuing maintenance or continuation treatment, and more than 80 percent experience recurrence within three years (Fava & Kaji, 1994). Not surprisingly, maintenance therapies have become increasingly important, particularly for patients at high risk for relapse.

1. Evaluate depressed patients for high-risk factors for relapse and recurrence.

Fava and Kaji (1994) profile the depressed patient risk for relapse. Relapse predictors include: (1) chronicity of the illness, three or more previous episodes; (2) those with double depression, i.e., major depression superimposed over dysthymia; (3) those with a long duration of index or first depression prior to assessment and treatment; (4) the presence of persistent or residual symptoms; (5) single or unmarried status; (6) persistent negative self-appraisal; (7) younger age; and (8) those with a greater degree of neuroticism and personality disorder traits. Hooley and Teasdale (1989) have studied relapse in married depressed patients. They find that several factors predict relapse, but the single best predictor is the patient's response to the question: "How critical is your spouse of you?" Patients who relapsed had highly critical spouses.

2. Incorporate relapse prevention intervention for depressed patients, particularly those with risk factors for relapse.

Cognitive therapy and other problem-focused treatment approaches tend to incorporate relapse prevention strategies as part of the treatment process. Rush and Hollon (1991) report that when cognitive therapy is combined with medication, cognitive therapy provides protection against relapse. This is the case even when medication has been stopped.

Serotonergic agents have recently gained considerable popularity in the long-term treatment of depression. This is largely due to the limited side-effect profile of these agents. However, recent data suggest that long-term treatment with these agents may require higher rather than lower doses, as compared to those utilized during the acute phase of treatment. This, of course, is the opposite of treatment with tricyclic agents.

PATIENT RESOURCES

Nontechnical Books

There are a few highly regarded nontechnical books that have been regularly recommended by clinicians to their patients. The first two have achieved the status of "classics."

- *Feeling Good: The New Mood Therapy* (1991), by David Burns, M. D. New York: Signet (paperback).
- *Control Your Depression* (1978), by Peter Lewisohn, Ph.D. et al. Englewood Cliffs, NJ: Prentice-Hall.
- *Feeling Good Handbook* (1991), by David Burns, M. D. New York: Signet (paperback).

Support Groups

The National Depressive and Manic Depressive Association (NDMDA) has local chapters throughout the U.S. and Canada. The NDMDA has an annual conference, a newsletter, a resource center, and audio and video materials for educating families and the community about depressive disorders. They sponsor community support groups for depressed patients and their families in most communities. Contact NDMDA at 730 North Franklin Street, Suite 501, Chicago, IL 60610; tel. (312) 642-0049; FAX (312) 642-7243, for information on resources, conferences, newsletters, and support-group locations.

12

Schizophrenia

Schizophrenia and its treatment can be conceptualized with a stress-vulnerability coping model wherein the schizophrenic patient is genetically vulnerable to schizophrenic decompensation when stresses outweigh protective coping factors. Biological protective factors include compliance with neuroleptic medication, social protective factors include peer social support and functional supportive families, and psychological protective factors include adequate personal and interpersonal coping skills (Fallon & Liberman, 1983). This model provides the clinician with several avenues of intervention, such as ensuring optional medication treatment, decreasing destructive family interactions, and improving the patient's ability to cope with the symptoms and deficits associated with schizophrenia. Combining treatment modalities in these three areas may well be necessary to achieve effective treatment outcomes.

Most schizophrenic patients treated in outpatient settings will benefit from combined treatment. In the past, researchers addressed the question of whether psychotherapy or other psychosocial interventions could be substituted for medication. Overwhelmingly, these studies found that patients who were not adequately stabilized on medication were unable to benefit from psychosocial treatments. On the other hand, there is a growing consensus that schizophrenic patients who have been stabilized on medication reap considerable benefits from appropriate psychosocial treatment. Complicating treatment planning for chronic schizophrenic patients are issues of noncompliance, and especially relapse and recurrence of acute symptoms that create havoc for patients, families, and clinicians.

Because of the severity and chronicity of this disorder, the effectiveness of combined treatment is influenced by the timing of each treatment, the drug dosage and intensity of the treatment, the adverse effects associated with the combined modalities, and the selection of patients for the particular combined modalities. Because psychosocial modalities can be quite different in content and therapeutic focus, it is not possible to make broad generalizations about the result of these nonmedication modalities and their interactive effects with the standard neuroleptics or the newer agents: respiridone and clozapine. This brief chapter will, however, provide treatment guidelines based on current research. These guidelines involve three types of combined modalities, various means of incorporating psychoeducation and social skill training, including medication groups, and a number of recommendations for dealing with two major issues in the outpatient treatment of schizophrenia: compliance and relapse.

COMBINED TREATMENT IS ESSENTIAL FOR THE MAJORITY OF SCHIZOPHRENIC PATIENTS

According to the "rule of thirds," one-third of all individuals diagnosed and hospitalized with schizophrenia recover completely, one-third need ongoing treatment and occasional hospitalization, and one-third remain unimproved (Torrey, 1983). Even though recent changes in diagnostic criteria and the introduction of promising treatments may modify this "rule" somewhat, schizophrenia is often a devastating, lifelong illness marked by exacerbations and remission. Research suggests this illness is more likely to respond to multimodal rather than to single-modality treatment. Considered here are guidelines for combining individual psychotherapy and medication management, family therapy and medication, group therapy and medication, and other combinations of these modalities.

1. Schizophrenic patients can profit from focused individual psychotherapeutic intervention.

Although most schizophrenics are unsuitable for traditional psychodynamic psychotherapy, the judicious use of tailored psychotherapeutic technique is essential to engage resistant and medication noncompliant patients to accept medical intervention. Although brief sessions of 15–30 minutes may be scheduled, an outpatient program that is sufficiently flexible can effectively serve this patient population. This is especially true if occasional unscheduled briefer contacts and phone calls are possible. The inability of many chronic patients to tolerate or benefit from the traditional 50–minute hour prompts this briefer, more flexible approach.

The course of treatment should be marked by the clinician's focus on the rational part of the patient's mind. Rather than exploring affects or delusional material, the clinician emphasizes the rational and healthy aspects of the patient's mind, as well as the measure of actual control that the patient has over his or her life. Thus, the clinician avoids direct challenges to the patient's psychotic belief system, utilizes reality testing and psychoeducation, and avoids emotional, stressful topics. Furthermore, a cautious optimism for the treatment of this disorder must be communicated by the clinician to the patient. The patient's refusal to take medication is viewed as resistance that needs to be explored. Does it originate from side effects, from psychotic beliefs, or from the patient's personality structure? Rather than allowing transference and countertransference to destroy treatment, the clinician must exhibit a willingness to compromise and negotiate, while sustaining the goal of the therapeutic alliance (Sarti & Cournos, 1990).

2. There are some specific indications for combining medication and group therapy with schizophrenic patients.

Group therapy has been shown to be quite effective with schizophrenic patients in increasing social relatedness, medication compliance, and treatment adherence, and learning social skills (Konas, 1993). The type of group–homogeneous or heterogeneous–seems to influence the outcome. The question of whether schizophrenic patients should be involved in groups consisting of diagnostically similar patients or in groups that also involve nonpsychotic members has yet to definitively answered. Those advocating heterogeneous groups note that such groups permit psychotic patients to join with reality-oriented, nonpsychotic patients and that such groups more closely reflect life outside the group. Konas (1993) indicates that heterogeneous groups may be best utilized with schizophrenic patients who are sufficiently stable to tolerate anxiety-producing feedback from others and who can tolerate and commit to involvement in a long-term outpatient group that meets weekly for 60–90 minutes. In short, heterogeneous groups are for the relatively higher-functioning and stable schizophrenic patient and thus have limited applicability to this patient population. Heterogeneous groups tend to follow an interpersonal or psychodynamic model (Vinagradov & Yalom, 1989).

Homogeneous groups should involve patients with schizophrenic disorders as well as those with schizoaffective disorders. These groups have less restrictive entrance requirements than heterogeneous groups and so have greater applicability to this patient population. Perhaps the only contraindication for this type of group is the patient who is so disruptive or psychotic that he/she cannot follow the discussion.

3. Combining medication and family intervention strategies is probably the most efficacious combined treatment for schizophrenic patients.

This combination of modalities is one of the earliest, as well as one of the most effective. Sufficient research has been done to be able to specify the type of family intervention most helpful during different phases of the illness (Wynne, 1983). For example, during the crisis period when the patient is actively psychotic and may need hospitalization, the family should be involved to facilitate crisis resolution, that is, getting the patient to take medication or be admitted to the hospital. The acute psychotic phase may last for several days, and although conjoint family sessions may be contraindicated as being too stimulating for the patient, family members shouldn't be automatically ruled out. However, during the subsequent subacute phase as positive symptoms subside, conjoint sessions are most fitting.

In the subchronic phase when the negative symptoms of schizophrenic are prominent–for example, lack of initiative, apathy, and perhaps medication noncompliance–family involvement takes the form of providing information, support, and establishing a compliance and relapse prevention plan. Psychoeducational approaches are best initiated at this point. These include family support groups, educational workshops, and the like. Guideline #3, "Incorporating Psychoeducational Methods in the Treatment of Schizophrenia," will elaborate this discussion. Generally speaking, traditional forms or systems of psychodynamic family therapy are no longer considered useful for the majority of schizophrenic patients. Instead, psychoeducation family interventions are considered the treatment of choice (Glick, Clarkin, & Goldsmith, 1993).

SINCE MEDICATION NONCOMPLIANCE IS A MAJOR TREATMENT ISSUE, ENHANCING AND MAINTAINING COMPLIANCE HAS TO BE A CENTRAL PART OF THE TREATMENT PLAN.

Noncompliance with medication regimens for schizophrenic outpatients shows a medium rate of 41 percent with oral neuroleptics. Noncompliance with long-acting depot neuroleptics is also surprisingly high (Young, Zonana & Shepler, 1986). Factors accounting for noncompliance range from psychotic ideation to rational responses and include thought disturbance, grandiosity, hostility, denial of illness, chronicity, paranoia, side effects, lack of drug efficacy, and a desire to be in control (Sarti & Cournos, 1990). The following specific guidelines are suggested.

1. Monitor the patient's subjective response to neuroleptics.

Research shows consistently that patients who do not fare subjectively well on medication are less likely to take them (Awad, 1993). Thus, it is recommended that the clinician pay close attention to patients' self-reports on how they feel taking the medication and whether their medication agrees with them. If patients report that they feel awful or like zombies, or that they can't think straight, or that the medication makes them feel worse, especially dysphoric, they will request a medication change, press for discontinuation of medication, or simply stop the medications unbeknownst to the clinician. Awad (1993) reports that noncompliance can be predicted if a schizophrenic patient has a dysphoric response to medication. At least two valid and reliable, short, self-rating instruments are available, one being the 10-item "Drug Attitude Inventory" (Awad, 1993). The value of such an inventory is that a patient may be more willing to disclose negative subjective response in writing rather than verbally and face-to-face.

2. Identify and monitor the patient's use of alcohol and other substances.

There is a startlingly high correlation between alcohol and substance use and medication noncompliance. Pristach and Smith (1990) found that 72 percent of substance-abusing or dependent schizophrenic patients were medication-noncompliant prior to rehospitalization. Even those patients with no history of alcohol abuse or dependence admitted to drinking alcohol in the month prior to admission. Not surprisingly, those with alcohol abuse histories drank significantly more and more often than nonabusers. And, 62 percent specifically reported being noncompliant when drinking alcohol. Mason and Siris (1992) report that among schizophrenic patients with postpsychotic depression and/or negative symptoms, cocaine or cannabis abuse was highly correlated with medication noncompliance. Perhaps, such substance use and abuse may be related to untreated postpsychotic depression or to medication-induced dysphoria. Whatever the cause, the clinician would do well to monitor the patient's use of substances. Furthermore, because alcohol decreases serum levels of antipsychotic agents, patients may not have reached or maintained therapeutic effect. Thus, patients will discontinue medication, believing it is not effective when, in fact, they may need medication dosages considerably higher than normal maintenance doses.

3. Encourage family involvement in ensuring medication compliance.

Chapter 6 describes family compliance counseling strategies that can be quite useful with schizophrenic patients. Other types of family involvement regarding compliance are described under the following guideline.

INCORPORATING PSYCHOEDUCATIONAL METHODS IN THE TREATMENT OF SCHIZOPHRENIA

Four specific types of psychoeducation have proved effective with this patient population. They are: social skills training, family psychoeducational interventions, medication and symptom management groups, and community support groups.

1. Tailor social skills training in the treatment plan of schizophrenic patients based on their skill deficits.

Skill deficits range from personal self-care and self-management skills to interpersonal relationship skills. Examples of such interpersonal deficits include poor eye contact, inappropriate facial expressions, poor response timing, limited spontaneity in social interactions, poor interpersonal judgment, and the inability to recognize and respond to emotion in others (Marder et al., 1991).

When social skills training is combined with medication in schizophrenic patients, there is an additive effect over either treatment alone. Marder et al. (1991) report that a skill-training group focused on both medication management and symptom management greatly increased the knowledge level and social skills of patients; these increases were sustained over at least six months. Eckman et al. (1990) also showed that medication compliance was significantly increased by this same intervention. Chapter 7 describes these social skill-training modules.

2. Psychoeducational family intervention efforts are effective treatment adjuncts.

Perhaps one of the best known psychoeducational programs involving family members has been described and researched by Anderson et al. (1986). The outcome goals of this program are to reduce the patient's vulnerability to environmental stress through maintenance medication, and to stabilize the family environment by increasing knowledge, coping skills, and level of support of family members. These goals are achieved through a four-phase program that extends over a course of several years.

Phase I and II emphasize information and realistic attitudes toward the chronic illness, while Phase III focuses on family communication and problem-solving strategies. Phase IV involves either a maintenance modality or more extensive use of psychodynamic and family system strategies for restructuring family systems behavior. Research on this and other family psychosocial interventions has concluded that compliance is achieved and the patient and family functioning is improved. Not surprisingly, these interventions are time-intensive, costly, and difficult to implement (Glick et al., 1993).

Bisbee's (1991) *Educating Patients and Families about Mental Illness* is an excellent practical resource that is less extensive and intensive than Anderson's program, and is probably more suitable for most clinic programs. This and other family psychoeducational resources are further discussed in Chapter 7.

3. Refer chronic schizophrenic patients to medication groups.

Medication groups were initially established for patients beginning prescribed neuroleptic medication. Medication groups for chronic schizophrenic and schizoaffective disordered patients tend to be long-term, ongoing groups. The format for such groups, and their indications and contraindications are described in some detail in Chapter 7.

4. Encourage patient involvement in community support group.

Currently, schizophrenic patients in the U.S., many Canadian provinces, and some cities in Ireland and the United Kingdom can find support groups sponsored by Recovery, Inc. Recovery is probably the oldest patient-led support for psychiatric patients. Recovery is a system of self-help, aftercare technique developed by the late Abraham Low, M.D., a Chicago psychiatrist. Meetings are based on Low's method of "will training." Recovery's stated purpose is to help prevent relapse and forestall chronicity in psychiatric patients. Patients are expected to comply with medication and other treatment prescriptions, as well as practicing Recovery principles daily. Another community support group is Schizophrenics Anonymous, which is based on the 12-step philosophy.

RELAPSE PREVENTION IS A CRITICAL COMPONENT IN THE TREATMENT OF SCHIZOPHRENIA

Preventing relapse and recurrence in schizophrenia is a challenge, given that relapse rates are exceedingly high. Davis et al. (1993) report that *all* schizophrenic patients not treated with neuroleptics will relapse within three years. Goldstein (1991) reports that 30 percent of all patients on neuroleptics relapse during the first year, whereas about 70 percent of patients on placebo relapse during that same period. Hogarty (1984) reports that of those willing to take medication, approximately 40 percent relapse during the first year after hospital discharge, and 15 percent each year thereafter.

The goal of outpatient maintenance treatment with schizophrenic patients is to prevent relapse in order for the patient to function within the community. Three specific guidelines are offered: appropriate dosing, family involvement, and developing a personal relapse plan.

1. Achieve appropriate medication dosage.

Strategies for long-term medication maintenance have been advocated to reduce relapse. The two most commonly practiced are "targeted" or "intermittent" dosing and "lower dosing." In the targeted strategy, the patient is placed on a drug-free regimen after he or she becomes stabilized, and restarted on aggressive drug regimen only when prodromal signs appear. The lower-dosing strategy involves continuous use of medication, but at substantially lower doses than the previous stabilization dose. If and when prodromal signs occurred, higher doses were utilized and thereafter the lower dose was reinstituted (Goldstein, 1991).

There has been considerable research on these two strategies. Data now suggest that the "targeted" strategy results in very high levels of relapse and rehospitalization. Nevertheless, individuals on this dose strategy do experience fewer side effects. Not surprisingly, many patients prefer this maintenance schedule. The standard dose, i.e., the dose usage most commonly used in clinical practice, showed the lowest relapse rates. Furthermore, when patients are stabilized and on a moderate to low dose and have concurrent psychosocial treatment, there is very little difference in the side effects experienced (Schooler, 1994b). It may well be that the newer serotonin-dopamine antagonists such as clozapine and respiridone will decrease relapse rates to some degree, since these newer agents have limited side effect profiles, particularly extrapyramidal symptoms (EPS).

2. Involve the family whenever possible.

When the family members are available and committed to the patient's treatment plan, at a minimum the clinician should engage the family's assistance in recognizing prodromal signs. During the relatively symptom-free maintenance phase, the patient and family should be instructed about the relationship between neuroleptic dosage, the potential for relapse, and the appearance of side effects. And since most patients experience predictable mood and behavioral changes, i.e., warning symptoms, the family should be enlisted so that medication and psychosocial strategies can be quickly utilized to prevent the acute symptoms of psychosis. The symptom management module described in Chapter 7 teaches patients and family members to distinguish between warning symptoms, acute symptoms, and persistent symptoms. While persistent symptoms, i.e., chronic, subclinical symptoms, are not likely to precipitate relapse, they can result in endless requests for medication changes and may account for noncompliance. Strategies, such as distraction and activity, for dealing with persistent symptoms are also discussed in Chapter 7. Breier and Strauss (1983) describe various self-control strategies for persistent symptoms common in schizophrenic patients.

Schooler (1994a) reports that it does not really matter what or how intensive are the psychosocial or psychoeducational interventions that are utilized with patients and their families. All that seems to matter is that the family be engaged in the treatment process, as the family is such a key factor in treatment outcome.

Finally, Goldstein (1991) recommends that patients and families engage in anticipatory planning to prepare them for taxing events that might trigger relapse. Anticipatory planning includes identifying potential disruptive upcoming events and devising prevention and coping strategies for managing them.

3. Help the patient develop a personal treatment strategy for preventing relapse.

Hogarty (1993) suggests that each patient needs a personal plan tailored to his/her unique circumstances. Such a relapse prevention plan includes attention to the emotional environment at home and in treatment setting, coping skills, everyday stressors, and a realistic treatment plan. First, the patient and family need to create a stimuli-controlled environment that is safe and predictable. The family and patient need to learn day-to-day survival skills to cope with unexpected stressors. Clinicians need to be aware of and control their "expressed emotion" behaviors. Specifically, Hogarty refers to the clinician's withholding warmth or nurturance and expressing subtle dissatisfaction when the patient's performance does not meet treatment expectation. He also believes that treatment must be based on patient and family goals that can be implemented in small steps. Finally, Hogarty assumes that the patient will take one step backward for each two steps forward.

PATIENT AND FAMILY RESOURCES

Reading Materials

- *Surviving Schizophrenia: A Family Manual* (1983), by E. Fuller Torrey, M.D. New York: Harper & Row (paperback and hardback).
- *How You Can Help: A Guide for Families of Psychiatric Hospital Patients* (1984), by Herbert Korpell, M.D. Washington, DC: American Psychiatric Press (paperback).

Community Support Groups

Information about Recovery Groups in your area can be found in the white pages of your telephone directory under "Recovery, Inc.–The Association of Nervous and Former Mental Patients" or by writing Recovery Headquarters, 802 N. Dearborn Street, Chicago, IL 60610, or calling (312) 337-5661.

13

Personality Disorders

Personality-disordered patients represent different things to different clinicians. For many they are a nightmare, whereas for others they are just another therapeutic challenge. The fact is that there is mounting optimism about the treatability of personality disorders–not just the management of these disorders, but their treatability. Stone (1993) designates the DSM personality disorders into three categories: "typically amenable to treatment," which includes the avoidant, dependent, histrionic, and obsessive compulsive disorders; the "intermediate treatability," which includes borderline, narcissistic, and schizotypal personality disorders; and "scarcely or non-amenable to treatment," which includes antisocial, paranoid, passive aggressive, and paranoid personality disorders. Surprising to many is Stone's designation of the borderline personality disorder in the category of "intermediate treatability" rather than "non-amenable" to treatment. Nevertheless, controlled research studies clearly support Stone's contention about the treatability of this disorder (Linehan, Heard & Armstrong, 1993).

This chapter provides a brief overview of the three clusters of the DSM-IV personality disorders, emphasizing general strategies and specific treatment guidelines for the "amenable to treatment" and "intermediate treatability" personality disorders. Because of the particular challenge it poses and because of the volume of research and clinical reports on it, the borderline personality disorder will be highlighted.

GENERAL TREATMENT STRATEGIES

1. Perform a comprehensive diagnostic evaluation with particular attention to pattern and level of functioning.

As with other disorders in Part II of this book, an extensive and comprehensive evaluation is essential. Of the five P's of the psychiatric formulation, "pattern" is the most important. In the context of personality disorder, "pattern" refers to the predictable manner of responding to triggering events. Pattern reflects the individual's schemas, styles and skill deficits. Schemas refer to the basic belief structures involving selfview and worldview and are basic to psychodynamic and cognitive formulations of personality. Schemas of personality disorders resemble those that are triggered and activated in symptom disorders, but are continuously operative. For instance, in the dependent personality disorder, the schema "I must be helped" will be activated whenever a problematic situation arises, whereas in depressed persons it will be prominent only during the depressive episode (Beck et al., 1990).

Styles refers to the features of temperament that greatly influence behavior and functioning, such as impulsivity, hypersensitivity, and nonreactivity. The role of temperament in personality disorder is the basis of considerable theoretical and research focus today. Siever and Davis (1991) posit that there is an underlying biological or temperament basis for the personality disorders and propose four dimensions of psychopathology that relate a neurotransmitter system to specific clusters of personality disorders. The affective instability and impulsive aggressivity dimensions are believed related to cholinergic, adrenergic, and serotonergic systems that are reflected in the dramatic cluster. The anxiety inhibition dimension is related to autonomic nervous system and reflected in the anxious cluster, while the cognitive perceptual dimension is related to the dopaminergic system and reflected in the odd, eccentric cluster of personality disorders.

Skill deficits refer to the absence or limited development of basic life skills. Necessary life skills include assertive communication, negotiation, decision-making, problem-solving and self-management.

2. Combined treatment is the rule rather than the exception in the successful treatment of personality disorders.

Combining two or more treatment modalities is often necessary to effect change with personality disordered patients. Since the patient's maladaptive pattern is consistent and constant and reflects temperamental style and skill deficits as well as defective schemas, a single modality like insight-oriented individual psychotherapy, which primarily addresses schemas, is not likely to impact style or skill deficits. Even advocates of psychoanalytic psychotherapies recognize the value of and need for combined modalities (Stone, 1993; Winer & Pollock, 1989).

To mention the obvious, a coexisting Axis I disorder, especially an anxiety or depressive disorder, must be evaluated for pharmacotherapy. Even though there may be no obvious indication for the use of medication to modify style/temperament features, utilizing medication for the Axis I condition while directing other psychotherapeutic interventions to Axis II features represents combined treatment.

3. Emphasize compliance and relapse prevention in the course of treatment.

By definition, the maladaptive patterning of the personality disorders is constant and pervasive, unlike the acute or episodic nature of the symptoms disorders. Personality disordered patients easily slip back into familiar but maladaptive affective, cognitive, behavioral, and interpersonal patterns. Initial effort to change these patterns is typically resisted. Not surprisingly, treatment adherence, including medication noncompliance, is usually a major issue with these patients. Throughout the course of treatment, relapse prevention must be promoted. Some would argue that if such patients do not become aware of their vulnerabilities and high-risk situations and triggering events, the clinician has been remiss! Booster sessions and other relapse prevention strategies can be effective in keeping the patient from resuming maladaptive patterns (Wilson, 1992).

DRAMATIC CLUSTER PERSONALITY DISORDERS

The DSM-IV Axis II dramatic cluster consists of the antisocial, borderline, histrionic, and narcissistic disorders. Stone (1993) contends that all but the antisocial personality disorder are amenable to treatment. The borderline, histrionic, and narcissistic disorders share many common features and often coexist in patients. They are also referred to as the "self disorders" (Gunderson, 1988). Furthermore, they are the most frequently encountered personality disorders in outpatient psychiatric settings and provide some of the most difficult clinical challenges to treatment staffs. Because of their tendency to deny responsibility for their problems and their dramatic and impulsive style, these patients engender transference and countertransference problems unlike those of any other type of patient. Readers wishing additional information on the description, diagnosis, formulation, and combined treatment strategies of these disorders is referred to Sperry (1995) *Handbook of Diagnosis and Treatment of the DSM-IV Personality Disorders.*

Histrionic Personality Disorder

Patients with this disorder are self-dramatizing, seductive, attention-seeking, and exhibitionistic. They show a driven quality to emotional displays and a desperate need to attract affection and attention. Others tend to experience this desire for affection as shallow and manipulative. In terms of style and skill deficits, they exhibit exaggerated and excitable affects, demanding, self-indulgent behavior, and a cognitive style characterized as global, vague, andgullible (Shapiro, 1965).

Narcissistic Personality Disorder

Patients with this disorder lack empathy, are grandiose, and are hypersensitive to evaluation by others. Exploitation and entitlement are characteristic of their pattern. These patients look inward for gratification and reinforcement, while dependency on others is very threatening and constitutes "narcissistic injury." Negative evaluation typically leads to rage, shame, and denial, which are projected onto others in the guise of splitting and projective identification. In terms of style and skill deficits they exhibit overmodulation of negative effect, exhibit nonempathic and exploitable, noncooperative behavior, and utilize a cognitive style characterized by entitlement and self-deception.

Borderline Personality Disorder

The borderline personality has been described as a decompensated variant of the dependent, histrionic, or narcissistic personality (Millon, 1981). Impulsivity and emotional instability characterize this disorder. Borderline patients experience great difficulty maintaining a stable, cohesive sense of identity, largely because they failed to form a coherent and integrated set of self schemas. Self-destructive behavior, including parasuicidal behavior, is common. In terms of style and skill deficits, mood instability and feelings of emptiness and inability to tolerate frustration characterize their affect; self-destructive actions and social and occupational underachievement characterize their behavior; and impulsivity and splitting characterize their cognitive style and functioning.

TREATMENT GUIDELINES FOR DRAMATIC CLUSTER PERSONALITY DISORDERS

1. Combined treatment is generally indicated when marked skill-deficit, lower functioning, or symptomatic style features are present.

For the dramatic cluster disorder, group or family modalities are often readily acceptable to the patient as adjuncts to individual psychotherapy. The degree of readiness for treatment must be assessed at the outset of treatment and monitored thereafter, as histrionic and borderline patients tend to gravitate to psychiatric treatment to get attention and feel better, but not necessarily to make changes. Unlike patients with Odd and Anxious Cluster disorder who hesitate to come for treatment, narcissistic, borderline, and histrionic patients generally enter treatment for symptom relief more easily. But whether or not they stay in treatment–especially narcissistic personality disordered patients, who commonly depart therapy when their narcissistic injury is soothed–and engage in the difficult work of personal growth is largely a function of level of readiness for change.

2. Utilize behavioral, cognitive, or psychoeducational strategies for skill deficits.

Since skill deficits tend to be a significant impediment to higher levels of functioning, it is necessary to reverse these deficits. When role playing and modelling the specific prosocial behavior is insufficient, formal social skill training must be implemented inside or outside the individual treatment context. Homogeneous groups are particularly useful for social skills training of borderline and histrionic patients.

3. Utilize focused therapeutic interventions to modify dysfunctional schemas.

Both psychodynamic and cognitive therapies have been shown to be effective in modifying core schemas. Turner (1992) describes Dynamic-Cognitive Behavior Therapy (DCBT), which he believes is specifically geared toward the dramatic impulsive personality disorders. DCBT integrates dynamic strategies to modify the patient's dysfunctional schemas, specifically interpretive techniques to break through to change and interpret conflict. It also utilizes cognitive and behavioral strategies to modify complicated distortions and contain impulsive and self-harming behavior.

4. Utilize medication strategies to modify and reduce symptomatic, targeted style features.

Siever and Davis (1991) contend that of the four dimensions of personality psychopathology, the affective instability dimension and the impulsivity/aggression dimension are the essential disturbances in the dramatic cluster. Other stylistic features associated with the dramatic cluster are interpersonal sensitivity and transient psychotic symptoms. For borderline patients, lithium and carbamezapine have been effective for affective instability, while serotonergic agents have been effective with impulsivity and aggressivity. Low-dose neuroleptics have been shown to be useful for transient psychotic features (Coccaro & Kavoussi, 1991). Siever (1993) reports that serotonergic agents, like fluoxetine and sertraline, are effective for reducing the interpersonal sensitivity and reactivity commonly noted in narcissistic and histrionic personalities. Finally, serotonergic agents have some efficacy in lower-functioning histrionic patients exhibiting impulsivity and affective instability.

GUIDELINES SPECIFIC TO BORDERLINE PERSONALITY DISORDERS

1. Carefully consider indications and contraindications for combined treatment.

Combined treatment for borderline patients is indicated for those with severe symptoms for which symptom relief has been slow with psychosocial treatment; for those with overmodulated affects; for those with impulsive aggressivity; and for those with transient psychotic regression. These patients should have combined medication and individual therapy. Similarly, borderline patients with significant interpersonal disturbance and identity issues should be considered for combined medication, individual, and group treatment modalities. Furthermore, to increase medication compliance and to more accurately assess the effects of medication, conjoint treatment in which family sessions or sessions with a significant other, roommate, or job supervisor should also be considered.

Contraindications to combined treatment include a variety of patient presentations. Patients with high overdose potential who cannot be controlled with limit setting are probably not candidates for combined individual and medication treatment. Group treatment, including partial hospitalization, may be an alternative. Patients who may be responsive to medication but have a history of negative therapeutic reactions probably should not be offered individual psychotherapy. The "no treatment option" (Frances, Clarkin & Perry, 1984) should be considered instead. Similarly, patients who utilize medication to precipitate crises in therapy or where medication becomes the central focus of therapy probably should not be offered combined treatment (Koenigsberg, 1993).

2. Combining family therapy with medication has considerable advantage.

Research indicates that families of borderline patients also demonstrate increased impulsivity and affective instability as well as significant problems with individuation, boundary violations, and enmeshment (Glick, Clarkin, & Goldsmith, 1993). Therefore, involving the borderline patient's family or spouse can be useful in decreasing enmeshment, respecting boundaries, and facilitating individuation. Family therapy can also increase overall family functioning and communication, provide education about the nature of the disorder, and support compliance with medication or other treatment modalities. To the extent that the family is motivated and has some capability of modulating affects and controlling projections, they may be a helpful adjunct to the overall treatment plan. Glick et al. (1993) suggest that a mixture of systems, psychodynamic, behavioral, and psychoeducational family therapy intervention is preferable to a single approach to family therapy.

3. Recognize and anticipate transference and countertransference complications.

A variety of transference phenomena are common with borderline patients. Patients with a history of transference enactments should probably be offered a trial of medication prior to the introduction of intensive individual psychotherapy to avoid or reduce such enactments.

Otherwise, the clinician should consider utilizing a structured medication management protocol in an individual format.

Issues of splitting are particularly common with borderline patients when medication is monitored by one clinician and psychotherapy is provided by another. However, splitting can also become manifest when the prescribing clinician further provides formal psychotherapy. In the case of two clinicians, when both clinicians are able to integrate psychological and biological perspectives and regularly collaborate with one another to present a "united front," splitting can be reduced or eliminated (Woodward, Duckworth, & Guthiel, 1993). When there is a single clinician, splitting is possible only when the clinician has a split view, i.e., biological vs. psychological, of treatment. Further complicating the matter is the task differential between prescribing medication and practicing psychotherapy. While psychotherapy favors spontaneous discourse and activity on the part of the patient, medication monitoring is much more directive and requires considerable clinician activity. Since borderline patients may find it disruptive and difficult to move between these two tasks, it can be useful to set aside a few minutes at the beginning of a session to review medication effects and arrange for prescription, and then shift to the more obvious psychotherapeutic mode of discourse (Koenigsberg, 1993).

Medication compliance is often a problem in combined treatment with borderline patients, especially when medication is perceived by the patient as a chemical means by which the clinician can exert control over the patient's mind and will. Thus, medication compliance can be viewed as acquiescing to the control of the clinician, while noncompliance is viewed as taking back that control. For this reason, it is important for the clinician to elicit specific fantasies the patient has about medication and its effects, as well as the meaning of medicating the patient for the clinician in the countertransference (Koenigsberg, 1991). The interested reader is referred to Koenigsberg (1991, 1993) for a more detailed discussion of combined treatment issues with borderline patients.

THE ANXIOUS CLUSTER PERSONALITY DISORDERS

The Anxious Cluster consists of the avoidant, dependant, and obsessive compulsive personality disorders: Stone (1993) considers each of these disorders as "typically amenable to treatment." Siever and Davis (1991) describe the anxiety/inhibition dimension of personality psychopathology as underlying the anxious cluster. They suspect that the etiology for these dimensions is a disturbance in autonomic functioning. Traditionally, the anxious cluster of disorders has not been considered amenable to medication treatment and was usually treated with insight-oriented psychotherapy. Recently, however, there is increased support for the use of medication with the avoidant personality disorder, and the utilization of cognitive behavioral therapy with all three disorders.

The Dependent Personality Disorder

Patients with this disorder tend to be quite passive, nonassertive, and overly submissive and pleasing. Typically, they are insecure, anxious, preoccupied with fears of abandonment, and indecisive. Their schema involves a self-view characterized by personal inadequacy, and they see the world as entitlement to be cared for because of their inadequacy. In terms of style and skill deficits, they are likely to have affects characterized by anxiety, hypersensitivity to disapproval, and fear of abandonment. Their behavioral style is characterized by passive acquiescence, clinging to others for reassurance, and indirectly demanding that others make decisions for them. Cognitively, they tend to be self-effacing, uncritical, and highly suggestible.

The Obsessive-Compulsive Personality Disorder

Patients with this disorder are preoccupied with orderliness and perfectionism. They are also dependable, loyal, and polite, while being somewhat rigid and nonspontaneous. Their schemas involve a self-view of being responsible for anything that might go wrong, and a view of the world in which life is unpredictable and people are irresponsible. In terms of style and skill deficits, their affective style is characterized by emotional constriction and avoidance of feelings, although they are capable of harboring enormous amounts of anxious, angry feelings. Their behavioral and interpersonal style is marked by social inhibition and an overconcern for trivial details and meticulousness. Cognitively, their style is inflexible, rule-focused, and restrictive such that they have considerable difficulty making decisions and prioritizing.

The Avoidant Personality Disorder

Patients with avoidant personality disorder exhibit a pervasive pattern of social inhibition, feelings of inadequacy, and hypersensitivity to negative evaluation. Thus, they tend to have limited social networks and have difficulty relating with and trusting others because they fear rejection. Their schemas involve a self-view of inadequacy and unlikableness, and a view of people as critical. Thus, they view the world as unfair, alongside a demand that others like and accept them. In terms of style and skill deficits, their affective style can be characterized as shy, tense, and apprehensive, and hypersensitive to potential rejection and humiliation. Their behavior and interpersonal style are characterized by social withdrawal and contingent personal relation ships. Their cognitive style is one of vigilance and self-doubt as they scan their emotional environment looking for clues of unconditional acceptance or potential rejection.

TREATMENT GUIDELINES FOR THE ANXIOUS CLUSTER PERSONALITY DISORDER

Unlike the situation with the dramatic-compulsive cluster of personality disorders wherein those disorders not only tended to coexist in a patient but style features were often responsive to medication, inclusive treatment guidelines for personality disorders in the anxious cluster are not possible. Thus, this section briefly reviews separate treatment guidelines for each disorder.

1. Avoidant Personality Disorder

First consideration should be given to a medication evaluation for any coexisting Axis I disorder. With avoidant personality, an anxiety or depressive disorder is often present. And because generalized social phobia–as distinct from a focused social phobia, i.e., fear of public speaking–has been shown to overlap considerably with avoidant personality disorder, a medication trial should be routinely considered.

Deltito and Stam (1989) have shown the generalized social phobia/ avoidant personality disorder to be responsive to either phenelzine, an MAOI inhibitor, or fluoxetine. Liebowitz et al. (1991) have also shown that fluoxetine is effective with generalized social phobia/avoidant personality disorder, whereas a beta blocker is still the treatment of choice for discrete social phobia. Two new RIMAs, reversible inhibitors of monoamine oxidase A, broforomia, and moclobemide, may be particularly useful for this disorder because they do not require the dietary restrictions of the MAOIs. Currently, RIMAs are not approved for use in the United States.

Thus, one form of combined treatment involves medication and individual therapy. Because of the considerable social skill deficits, a behavioral or psychoeducational focus is usually necessary. Therefore, individual therapy must usually include behavioral or psychoeducational focus or skill-building, while also addressing the need for schema modification. For the lower functioning avoidant patient, adding group therapy is recommended (Alden, 1989). Similarly, if the patient is married, couples therapy may be added or replace the group component. Benjamin (1993) notes that intimacy and trust issues for the avoidant patient can be effectively addressed in couples therapy.

2. Dependent Personality Disorder

If no Axis I disorder coexists, medication has no current role in the treatment of dependent personalities. In fact, medications are contraindicated. Anxiolytics are likely to be abused by these patients and antidepressants are inappropriate for reactive symptoms (Reid, 1989).

On the other hand, other forms of combined treatment have a central role in the treatment of this disorder. Individual therapy focused on modifying schemas might be supplemented with cognitive behavioral or psychoeducational intervention targeted at skill deficits such as assertive communication, decision making, or negotiation. While these skills can be modelled and practiced in an individual format, a group format is advantageous. Marital or couples therapy could also be considered. A unique combining of group and couples therapy has been described by Barlow and Waddell (1985) in which spouses with dependent personalities and panic-agoraphobia are treated along with their spouse in a structured group setting.

3. Obsessive-Compulsive Personality Disorder

There is currently no indication for the use of medication with this disorder, unless there is a concurrent Axis I. While clinical lore suggests that this personality disorder commonly coexists with Obsessive-Compulsive Disorder (OCD), research does not support this belief. Actually, OCD is more likely to occur with dependent and avoidant personality disorders than with obsessive compulsive personality disorder (Baer & Jenike, 1992).

Nevertheless, combined treatment is central to the successful treatment of this disorder (Salzman, 1989). Because of the dominance of style/temperament features and skill deficit in this disease, behavioral interventions are essential. Schema modification is less likely to occur when one uses a traditional nondirective psychodynamic approach. Salzman (1989) details the modifications of the psychodynamic approach that are necessary. Furthermore, he describes how psychodynamic individual and group treatment incorporating some behavioral methods can be combined. Wells et al. (1990) describe a combined approach integrating dynamic, cognitive, and interpersonal interventions in a group therapy context. Sperry (1995) suggests that when isolation of affect or perfectionism is the dominant presentation, a group modality such as described by Wells et al. (1990) can be particularly effective, whereas when indecisiveness is the dominant feature, an individual modality integrating dynamic and behavioral strategies is preferable.

THE ECCENTRIC CLUSTER PERSONALITY DISORDERS

The Eccentric Cluster consists of the schizoid, paranoid, and schizotypal personality disorders. According to Siever and Davis (1991), the disorders in the eccentric cluster probably result from disturbances in the dopaminergic system. Stone (1993) considers the schizotypal personality disorder as the only disorder in this cluster to be even partially amenable to treatment, even though it is a schizophrenic spectrum disorder. Interestingly, next to the borderline personality disorder, the schizotypal personality disorder has been the most researched

Axis II disorder. Accordingly, this section briefly describes the schizotypal personality and some treatment guidelines.

Schizotypal Personality Disorder

Patients with this disorder display a pervasive pattern of social and interpersonal deficits marked by acute discomfort and a reduced capacity for close relationships. They also exhibit cognitive and perceptual distortions and eccentricities of behavior. Their schemas involve a self-view of being quite different and estranged from others, and a view of the world that is dangerous, strange, and mysterious. In terms of style and skill deficits, their affective style is characterized as cold, aloof, and constricted. Their behavioral and interpersonal style can be described as eccentric, peculiar, and socially avoidant, along with a hypersensitivity to real or imaginary slights. Their cognitive style is ruminating and scattered and marked by magical thinking and superstition. Though depersonalization and derealization are often present, frank delusions and hallucinations are absent.

GUIDELINES FOR THE ECCENTRIC CLUSTER: SCHIZOTYPAL PERSONALITY DISORDER

1. **Combined treatment, especially medication and concurrent individual supportive psychotherapy, is the treatment of choice for this disorder.**
   Not surprisingly, since it is a schizophrenic spectrum disorder, schizotypal personality-disordered patients typically respond to medication.
2. **Because of the profound social skill defects, skill training is a useful adjunct to supportive psychotherapy.**
   This can be accomplished in an individual context, but seems to be more effective in a homogeneous group.
3. **Partial hospitalization or day hospital programs have been shown to be particularly advantageous with these patients.**
   Mehlum et al. (1991) propose that the structured social environment that characterizes day treatment programs is probably more

tolerable to these patients because it is much less intense than group therapy sessions that meet weekly.

4. **Low-dose neuroleptics seem to be the medication of choice for this disorder.**
   Although there are case reports suggesting the value of anxiolytics, amoxapine, and fluoxetine in this disorder, several placebo-controlled trials show consistently that low-dose neuroleptics are more beneficial for schizotypal patients with moderate to severe presentations. It is hypothesized that neuroleptics modify the cognitive-perceptual style/temperament features of this disorder (Siever & Davis, 1991).

PATIENT AND FAMILY RESOURCES

Reading Materials

Personality Self-Portrait (1990), by John Oldham, M.D., and Luis Morris (New York: Bantam).

There are few popular books on the various personality disorders that can be recommended to patients and their families. This is the exception. The authors distinguish personality styles from personality disorders–in DSM-III-R terms–and provide advice that is practical, well informed, and nonpatronizing.

Part IV

Special Applications

14

Inpatient Treatment

H. Steven Moffic, M.D., and
Kathryn Krieg, M.D.

In recent years, the nature of inpatient treatment has been changing dramatically, especially in the private sector. Lengths of stay have been rapidly decreasing, the goals of hospitalization have been changing, and the role of the psychiatrist has been affected (Munich & Gabbard, 1992). Lengths of stay commonly average seven days (somewhat higher for children and the elderly) with a treatment focus almost exclusively on the "medical necessity" for crisis resolution of high-risk situations rather than on character change or major symptom remission. Furthermore, the autonomy of psychiatrists has been significantly reduced through utilization review of their work. Reasons for these changes include the lack of research substantiating the value of longer stays (Gabbard, 1992), as well as major regional variations in lengths of stay (Rosenheck & Astrachan, 1990). As managed care has endeavored to reduce unnecessary costs and presumably maintain quality, long inpatient stays have been gradually reduced in an uncontrolled attempt to see if shorter stays or alternatives to hospitalization were clinically adequate.

The implications of these recent changes are still being formulated. Up to the late 1980s, solid studies on the outcome of managed care in general health care were virtually nonexistent (Gray & Field, 1989).

While there have been anecdotal reports of poor inpatient outcomes from shortened hospital stays, more recent studies seem inconclusive. On the other hand, one study found increased cost and poorer quality of care when patients were hospitalized later than it appeared they should have been for a variety of medical problems (Gonnella et al., 1990). Likewise, it was found that psychiatric inpatients who were discharged mainly due to economic considerations, such as managed care lack of authorization of payment, had poorer discharge planning and global outcome at six-month follow-up, but no increase in readmission rates (Sharfstein, 1992). Another uncontrolled study found that patients improved in several areas of psychosocial functioning with a brief hospitalization (Liberman et al., 1993). In another study done on hospitalized, depressed, elderly patients, before and after the implementation of the Medicare prospective payment system, the reduced length of stays was actually associated with improved quality of care (Wells et al., 1993).

Not surprisingly, this change in inpatient treatment has affected the role of the psychiatrist. While still a team leader to more of an extent than in most outpatient settings, the psychiatrist has become more of a collaborator and has focused on quicker outcomes in the inpatient setting. In many ways, the inpatient setting has become a testing ground for the unique training and expertise of the psychiatrist in maximizing and integrating psychotherapy and psychopharmacology in a cost-effective manner. Even though psychologists may be admitting patients and clinical nurse specialists prescribing medication at times, the special integrating role of the psychiatrist is still necessary. Briefer hospitalizations for sicker patients are calling for psychiatrists to maximize their particular expertise by using quicker–and possibly riskier–medication strategies and challenging them to adapt psychotherapy to this focus on quick symptom relief.

EVALUATION GUIDELINES

One key to keeping inpatient stays as short as possible is a thorough but focused evaluation. As much as possible should be done prior to the admission, including discussion of financial benefits, goals of the hospitalization, and projected length of stay. If at all feasible, patients should know their inpatient benefits at the time of insurance purchase or first outpatient contact, so they can begin to appreciate how that could influence inpatient treatment (Prezioso, 1994). One should be sure as much treatment was provided as possible on an outpatient basis, including day hospital, home visits, and even detoxification (Prezioso, 1994). Hospitalization can then be used when it is the only treatment setting where a combination of safety, understanding, and multimodal treatment would be available. Suicidal ideation by itself is therefore not a sufficient indication for hospitalization.

Additionally, this initial evaluation should include both focal and general data collection. Focal information should center on the specific reasons for hospitalization and attitudes toward treatment. Strengths and weaknesses in the patient and significant others for resolution of the admitting problems should be ascertained, including transference and countertransference tendencies. The more general data collection should involve ruling out conditions that might complicate treatment of the identified problem. Such conditions would include substance abuse, prior abuse or trauma, and personality traits. Such information can be obtained by the psychiatrist or staff specializing in such areas. In confusing diagnostic cases, rapid psychological testing can be cost-effective. The initial staffing with representatives of the treatment team should be done within the first two days. Likely indications for the need for more extended hospitalization include failure of prior brief hospitalizations, complicated problems involving a combination of high-risk Axis I and Axis II pathology, and nonsupportive, inadequate, or sabotaging environmental factors (Gabbard, 1992).

GENERAL TREATMENT GUIDELINES

In stark, practical terms, the main goal of hospitalization is discharge as soon as possible (Sederer, 1992). In order for the patient to achieve discharge, usually the admitting problem needs significant alleviation, whether that be suicidal risk, homicidal risk, severe psychosis, inability to care for oneself, or failed outpatient treatment. To help focus the patient on discharge, treatment should concentrate on the reason for admission and, as soon as possible, the patient should be given an estimated length of stay. Providing an estimated length of stay, similar to estimating the number of sessions for brief therapy, helps keep the inpatient on target, reduces secondary gain, and can lessen the impact of leaving.

In maximizing the use of psychopharmacology and psychotherapy for cost-effective hospitalizations, various strategies can be employed by the psychiatrist. For medication, strategies to increase the rapidity of response are important to consider, including loading doses (at least for adults) of lithium, valproic acid, neuroleptics, and nortriptyline. The main goal of medication in a brief hospitalization is toleration of the medication and some sense of beginning symptom relief. Psychotherapy should focus on the issues resulting in hospitalization and how to begin to handle things differently. If psychotherapy was not going well before hospitalization, psychotherapy consultation to the psychotherapist is a reasonable goal. Other than in failed intensive outpatient or brief hospitalizations, intensive psychodynamic psychotherapy is not indicated. For example, in suspected sexual abuse or Dissociative Identity Disorder, the goal of therapy would not be to integrate the personalities or recall all the major traumatic memories. Rather, the goal would be to prepare the patient for outpatient therapy, shore up adaptive defenses, and perhaps supplement with medication. These strategies may seem incomplete to many psychiatrists, especially those used to more extensive inpatient treatment, and as a consequence may be associated with increased anxiety in the psychiatrist concerning discharge.

To work expeditiously with reviewing entities, the psychiatrist needs to be able to provide clear information about the need for each inpatient day. The psychiatrist should personally see the patient daily, including weekends. Besides deciding on authorization of financial coverage, reviewing entities can also be helpful in suggesting and arranging resources. The unit milieu needs strong psychiatric leadership and should be accepting of limited goals and rapid turnover.

DISCHARGE GUIDELINES

Discharge planning with the patient should start within the first day or two, unless the patient is too psychotic to participate. Besides social worker collaboration with the patients, a hospital group devoted to discharge is most helpful. Involving social support for aftercare, especially with children, adolescents, and geriatrics, is often crucial for expeditious discharge. Such social support may include home health care provided through various organizations, which can decrease hospital stays. Aftercare treatment options should be considered and processed as the patient is improving. Although its necessity is often questioned by managed care reviewers, a trial pass can be helpful to substantiate readiness for discharge in uncertain cases. Continuity of care is important, whether that be with a prior clinician or to continue the inpatient thrust of treatment.

With the trend toward brief hospitalization, the psychiatrist needs to be even more wary of premature flight to health or pseudo-improvement. Someone with substance abuse problems may try to appear improved in order to quickly go back on the streets. A suicidally depressed patient may "improve" to the degree where he/she has more energy and focus to commit suicide. A psychotic patient may try to hide delusional thinking. In such cases, the psychiatrist needs to make a clear and financially convincing case for more hospital days, as longer treatment can not only produce more improvement but also reduce rehospitalization, save money in the longer run, and save lives. The appeal process should be pursued in disagreements as to authorization. Although the question of what is the legal responsibility of the managed care company versus the attending psychiatrist versus the hospital is still being processed, psychiatrists should ultimately make their discharge decisions on a clinical basis.

CHARTING

Traditionally, charting was done to summarize the evaluative, diagnostic, and treatment process. Included in the evaluation is the chief complaint, recent and past history, mental status, and formulation. Progress notes could be brief and just generally comment on progress. While such documentation is still necessary, additional charting is necessary to justify ongoing inpatient treatment under managed care review and must be clear to utilization reviews. This extra documentation for coverage needs to include comments on at least the following questions: What is the nature of the dysfunction? Why can't the treatment be provided at a lower level of intensity? Or, in other words, what can be done only in an inpatient setting? When will treatment on an inpatient level likely be completed? Where will treatment continue, and by whom?

In addition to proper charting, the attending psychiatrist may also need to verbally discuss the case with reviewers. Such verbal information must not contradict what is charted.

SPECIFIC TREATMENT GUIDELINES FOR MAJOR DEPRESSIVE DISORDERS

Hospitalization for Major Depression usually occurs only with a perceived suicidal risk or failed outpatient treatment with inability to function. Therefore, the usual inpatient treatment will focus on reducing suicidal risk and/or finding a new treatment plan that will work better. The expectation generally cannot be major symptom resolution, or to wait the usual 1–8 week period for the antidepressant to "kick in."

1. **If the major reason for hospitalization is suicidal risk, the psychotherapy approach is crucial to understand the dynamic issues producing the risk, whether that be undue guilt, unacceptable anger, or psychotic wishes (i.e., unification with a dead loved one).**
   Understanding the dynamics can allow the staff to focus on reducing the tendency toward suicide as a solution, such as better acceptance of anger, while leaving further insight and resolution to outpatient care. Interpersonal therapy to work on the social ramifications of the depression seems to produce an additive effect to medication.
2. **Medication should be used with efficacy, rapidity of therapeutic effects, and safety in mind.**
   As helpful and safe as the newer SSRIs have been for mild to moderately severe Major Depression and Dysthymia, it is much less clear that they are as successful in severe Major Depression (Goodwin, 1994). So far, there is also no apparent way to quicken the effects of SSRIs. At least for adults, an alternative inpatient strategy would be to use the older tricyclic antidepressants, especially nortriptyline (Warner, Griffin, & Peabody, 1993). While the suicide risk for overdose needs to be kept in mind for outpatient

follow-up, nortriptyline offers several particular inpatient advantages, including a possible therapeutic window that can be monitored with blood levels, useful supplementation with low-dose lithium (which may also protect against unanticipated manic swings), and the use of high initial doses to speed responsiveness. Using an initial loading dose of 75 to 125 mg at night often can significantly reduce depressive symptoms within one week. The main problematic side effect seems to be orthostatic hypotension, which can be treated with fludrocortisone. This strategy poses more cardiovascular and side-effect risks for children and the elderly. Unfortunately, there are as yet no comparable loading dose strategies for children or the elderly. For them, tricyclic antidepressants should be used in a more gradual fashion (with cardiovascular monitoring) or SSRIs can be used, keeping in mind the disparity in costs.

3. **When psychosis is involved, such as command hallucinations to hurt oneself, antipsychotic medication should be started first.**
   Once information is obtained as to its beginning effectiveness and side effects, an antidepressant should be added.
4. **When significant anxiety is present, brief usage of benzodiazepines will often be helpful.**
   Reduction of the anxiety will often reduce suicide risk and help the patient focus on the underlying issues.
5. **When the depression is postpartum, keeping the baby on the unit with the mother often speeds recovery.**
   Having the baby on the unit will provide a clearer picture of the nature of the developing relationship, and allow quicker addressing of the mother–child bond.
6. **For treatment failures or so-called treatment resistant depression, careful reassessment of diagnosis and adequacy of any prior treatment is crucial (Guscott & Grof, 1991).**
   New treatment strategies may include various medication changes, combinations, or augmentation, the provision of ECT, and a different psychotherapeutic approach.
7. **While the general expected length of stay can be 5–7 days, the presence of psychosis, dual diagnostic problems, unacceptable medication side effects, or lack of initial improvement can all delay the stay.**

These complicating factors should be addressed as quickly as possible, but not in a way that will make it impossible to tell what is affecting what. For instance, with the presence of psychosis, antipsychotic medication should be given first and quickly, then the antidepressant added after there is some sense of what the antipsychotic is doing.

SPECIFIC TREATMENT GUIDELINES FOR BIPOLAR DISORDERS

During depressive phases, hospitalization may be needed for the same reasons as Major Depression, although the symptoms may be somewhat different (sleeping too much rather than too little, eating more rather than less). For manic stages, hospitalization becomes necessary when the patient's behavior starts putting the patient or others at risk, often from doing dangerous things. Hospitalization is often difficult to achieve and maintain since the patient may enjoy how he/she feels during manic stages, so that the psychiatrist and family need to be firm and controlling.

1. **For manic stages, one can often accomplish rapid resolution of symptoms by loading doses of medication.**
   For purer appearing manic states, lithium is usually the drug of choice (Cummings et al., 1993); for mixed manic-like states, valproic acid 20 mg/kg/day can often achieve major resolution of symptoms within three days with minimal side effects (Keck et al., 1993).
2. **For depressed stages, medication would include any of the antidepressants plus mood stabilizers.**
   These two medications should be started together to avoid precipitation of mania by the antidepressant.
3. **Although psychotherapy is now known not to be the main treatment of choice in bipolar disorders, the psychiatrist can incorporate certain psychotherapeutic techniques that will supplement the medication and increase compliance (Kahn, 1990).**
   Although the psychiatrist cannot "talk" a patient out of an acute manic episode, clear limit-setting and education about what is happening to the patient can be useful. Family members should be

counselled to stay calm and avoid arguments with the patient. As the acute manic episode remits, helping the patient to understand the risks of desiring hypomanic states is important, as well as building realistic self-esteem.

4. **Especially for manic states, transference and countertransference problems should be watched for and handled.** The patient may often feel anger and fear at being controlled by medication and otherwise, while the psychiatrist may often feel anger and fear due to the patient's lack of control and gratitude for the psychiatrist's help. The psychiatrist needs to avoid trying to punish the patient in subtle ways, such as over- or undermedication, or letting the patient leave the hospital prematurely.

SPECIFIC TREATMENT GUIDELINES FOR SCHIZOPHRENIC DISORDERS

Hospitalization and rehospitalization for schizophrenia are quite common. Usually, the need arises from a worsening of psychotic symptoms, especially hallucinations, which will pose a risk to the well-being of the patient and others. For rehospitalization especially, the worsening often comes from the patient stopping medication. While most schizophrenic patients can benefit from a brief hospitalization, those with multiple previous hospitalizations–especially men–should be considered for lengthier hospitalization or a residential alternative (Appleby et al., 1993).

1. **Especially for exacerbations of psychosis, try to understand the causes, whether that be medication side effects, negative expressed emotion from the family, or too much intimacy.** Such understanding will indicate what problem needs to be addressed, both to reduce the psychosis and prevent future exacerbations.
2. **As in the emergency room setting, rapid tranquilizing can be helpful for more rapid resolution of symptoms, as well as for quickly ascertaining whether side effects will be a problem.** A dysphoric reaction from a reasonable stat intramuscular dose of a neuroleptic will often predict later poor compliance.

3. **For patients known to be poorly compliant due to neuromuscular side effects, the newer neuroleptics such as clozapine or risperadol are worth trying.**
   In using these newer neuroleptics, the increased cost of these medications must be kept in mind, and grants or medication studies used when available. Ultimately, the high cost of these medications may turn out to be less than repeated hospitalizations or intensive outpatient care.
4. **For patients known to be poorly compliant for other reasons, early hospital use of longer-acting intramuscular decanoate preparations is indicated.**
   With the intramuscular preparations, there will at least be 3–4 weeks of medication effects, which should help with the initial transition phase out of the hospital.
5. **A supplemental supportive psychotherapeutic approach that provides gentle reality testing for the patient, as well as an optimal emotional distance, is important.**
   With schizophrenic patients, too little closeness will evoke feelings of rejection, while too much closeness will be frightening. Brief sessions of 15–30 minutes that focus on practical issues are a helpful approach during the hospitalization.

SPECIFIC TREATMENT GUIDELINES FOR DISSOCIATIVE DISORDERS

Recent interest in Dissociative Disorders has led to the establishment of special inpatient units devoted to these disorders, with accompanying controversy over the need and long-term usefulness of inpatient treatment. While suicidal and homicidal behavior during dissociative episodes will often necessitate at least a brief hospitalization, the goal of hospitalization is often controversial. Whether and what kind of medication to use, as well as the kind of psychotherapy, continues to be researched. In addition, discovering dissociation from unsuspected sexual or physical abuse in patients with other disorders, especially presumed Depressive Disorders, will often complicate and lengthen the hospitalization by a few days.

1. **Medication should be used to treat specific target symptoms that pose high risk or interfere with psychotherapy (Putnam, 1989).**

Benzodiazepines should be used judiciously, due to the possible side effects of memory impairment in already compromised memory, but may be useful for nightmares and early stages of therapy when the patient is experiencing intense anxiety when trying to develop nondissociative methods of coping. Beta-blockers such as propranolol can be quite helpful in ameliorating violent behavior and reducing the frequency of dissociation, including rapid personality switching. Naltrexone is being studied for its effect on self-mutilating behavior and flashbacks (Bills & Kreisler, 1993). Antidepressants can help alleviate depression and thereby facilitate psychotherapy. Monoamine Oxidase Inhibitors are generally contraindicated due to the dietary risks during a dissociative episode.

2. **In using medication, placebo effects may be particularly strong because patients with Dissociative Disorders seem highly suggestible.**
   Too much suggestion about what the medication will do should be avoided.
3. **In those with different ego states, the effects of medication may vary in each state.**
   For instance, an antidepressant medication may seem to affect only one identity state and not the overall condition.
4. **The psychotherapeutic approach should be psychodynamic, with the main goal of hospitalization to establish or reestablish trusting in a therapist to begin to process or reprocess earlier trauma.**
   Hypnosis should be used sparingly and not to suggest other ego states. Caution should be used in immediately accepting the validity of traumatic memories.

SPECIFIC TREATMENT GUIDELINES FOR EATING DISORDERS

While hospitalization for Eating Disorders is sometimes necessary, precise indications for when and how long are lacking (Brotman, 1994). For Anorexia Nervosa, those who are less than 20% below average weight for height should be hospitalized if the patient does not seem motivated, has an uncooperative family, has physiological signs of risk, or has failed in less intensive treatment (American Psychiatric Association, 1993). For Bulimia Nervosa, hospitalization is needed much less often, but should be considered in suicidal patients, those having related life-threatening medical problems, or to break an out-of-control cycle unresponsive to outpatient treatment (American Psychiatric Association, 1993). Because many of the treatment strategies are geared specifically to these disorders, and because the patient can be so frustrating, inpatient staff should be well trained in eating disorders. A general medical ward should be used when the medical status is considered dangerous.

1. **Medication seems to have a limited role.**
   However, SSRIs have proven helpful at times, especially if depression, obsessiveness about eating, or compulsive behavior is still present after some improvement in eating behavior.
2. **In anorexic patients, hospitalization should focus on discharge target weights.**
   Expectations for reasonable weight gain, such as 1–3 pounds a week, should be communicated clearly and with the help of a dietician. A behavioral therapy approach, using positive and negative reinforcement, will help influence the behavior. Tube or parenteral feeding should be used only in life-threatening situations.
3. **In bulimic patients, careful monitoring and observation for bulimic behavior for two hours after meals are often essential to help break a serious binge–purge cycle.**
   Nutritional counselling and cognitive psychotherapy to reframe thinking about eating should supplement this behavioral approach.

SPECIFIC TREATMENT GUIDELINES FOR SUBSTANCE ABUSE DISORDERS

As a study of the Cleveland Admission, Discharge, and Transfer Criteria indicated, day treatment may often be as effective for those previously thought to need hospitalization (McKay, McLellan, & Alterman, 1992). Alcohol detoxification can be done on an outpatient basis with a motivated patient and helpful social network. Twenty-eight-day inpatient programs are becoming the exception for those who seem to fail other less intensive treatment programs. Generally, brief hospitalizations of 2–4 days are used for more controlled detoxification and to break through psychological resistance to treatment.

1. **Use medication for detoxification based on precise behavioral and physiological criteria understood by staff.**

Several protocols and guidelines are available, so one should be chosen that is well understood by all.

2. **Generally try to end the use of any potentially addictive medications before discharge.**
   For instance, the use of benzodiazepines should generally be stopped before discharge, and if necessary, carbomazepine used as a further transition.
3. **Carefully assess the patient's capacity to use self-help groups.**
   Not all patients will be comfortable with the spiritual and surrendering focus of AA-type groups.
4. **The psychotherapeutic endeavor in the hospital should focus on the role of substance use in the patient's life, including the beginning of the problem.**
   Understanding that will help the therapy focus on alternative problem-solving skills.

SPECIFIC TREATMENT GUIDELINES FOR BORDERLINE PERSONALITY DISORDER (AND OTHER PERSONALITY OR CONDUCT/OPPOSITIONAL DISORDERS)

Generally, these disorders include patterns of behavior that cause the patient—whether a child, adolescent, or adult—to have problems in getting along with others, but much of the behavior is ego-syntonic to the patient. Hospitalization should not be used to basically calm down those in the network or to punish the patient. Rather, it should be used when outpatient treatment is failing or for brief periods to reduce high-risk behavior.

1. **Medication should be used after a careful assessment and then cautiously geared to target symptoms (Swenson & Wood, 1990; Cowdry & Gardiner, 1988; Anselm, Nathan, et al., 1989).**
   Side effects are often particularly unwelcome to the patient with a Borderline Personality Disorder. Moreover, such patients will often split the medication from the psychotherapy, often devaluing one or the other (Koenigsberg, 1993).
2. **If psychotherapy is the main treatment approach, constant communication and agreement with the approach among staff are essential to avoid splitting of the staff.**
   Daily staff communication with the psychiatrist is important.

3. **If the patient has had a prior clinician, care should be made not to devalue the work of that clinician prematurely.** The goal of the hospitalization can be to consult with and advise the outpatient treatment program. If possible, the prior therapist can continue in the hospital.
4. **Generally, hospitalizations should be kept very brief or, in very selected cases, very long when more intensive psychotherapy in a safe, structured environment is necessary.** Regressive tendencies are common in borderline patients and must be watched for and addressed expeditiously.
5. **Significant others should be involved as much as possible, as sources of information and to help increase their therapeutic responsiveness to the patient.** Others can help verify or add to information from the patient. Helping others to understand the patient's tendencies may increase their patience.

CONCLUSION

Inpatient treatment continues to be the setting where the psychiatrist's unique ability to integrate psychotherapy and psychopharmacology is of crucial importance. However, the psychiatrist must be prepared to use these skills in a cost-effective manner, and be able to provide treatment in the tight space between unnecessary hospitalization and tardy hospitalization. The psychiatrist must be able to clearly state that the treatment can be provided only in an inpatient setting and is reasonably expected to produce improvement. To do so, the psychiatrist must be able to adapt traditional inpatient activities to the new managed care environment (Table 3). If able to do so successfully, such psychiatrists will be viewed as most valuable resources to provide quality treatment in a financially responsible manner.

TABLE 3
Changes in Inpatient Treatment

	Pre-Managed Care	*Managed Care*
LENGTH OF STAY	Weeks to months	Days to week or two
TREATMENT PLANNING	Therapy-oriented and/or problem-oriented	Goal-directed
DECISION MAKING	Psychiatrist in charge of team	Psychiatric team in conjunction with reviewing entity
CHARTING	Charting for clinical care	Charting for clinical care and for financial coverage
MEDICATION USE	Medication-free observation plus slow changes	Loading dose strategies and rapid changes
PSYCHOTHERAPY	Psychodynamic intensive therapy	Psychotherapy geared to crisis resolution and supporting medication use
GOALS	Removal of symptoms and/or character change	Reduction of risk and preparation for less intensive treatment

15

The Older Adult

Harold Harsch, M.D.

One of the basic tenets of geriatric medicine is that in the older adult many illnesses present with atypical clinical symptoms or may even lack expected cardinal symptoms (i.e., a urinary tract infection presenting as delirium). Moreover, the medical management of illness is often more complex due to the simple frailty that accompanies advancing age or the presence of multiple medical conditions–estimated at over 3.5 illnesses for the average elderly person living in the community (Wilson, Lawson, & Brass, 1962).

These tenets also apply to psychiatric illness in the older adult. The presentation of depression in the geriatric population often manifests itself with cognitive slowing and various somatic symptoms, rather than with the psychological sadness that often is seen in the younger individual. Several conditions such as stroke, primary degenerative dementia, and late-onset psychosis are primarily seen in the older adult. Clinical management of Axis I psychiatric conditions is more pharmacologically complicated because of acute or chronic medical conditions that are often present.

Psychiatric treatment of the older adult is also hampered by longstanding assumptions that view psychotherapy as less effective in older individuals. Are maladaptive coping styles more ingrained and unresponsive to treatment in the older adult? A literature search covering the last five years on psychotherapy and the elderly produced over 650 citations. Controlled studies, however, comparing and contrasting the various psychotherapeutic modalities in the elderly are still sparse, but all show efficacy for psychotherapeutic interventions.

There have been many advances in psychopharmacology over the past decade. These include the introduction of new psychoactive agents and an increase of our clinical knowledge of how to safely use drugs in the elderly. Much of our knowledge base, however, has come from small studies or individual experience. The majority of large drug studies have either excluded elderly patients or included only those without chronic medical conditions. This often leaves the geriatric clinician as the primary individual to closely monitor the older adult on multiple medications for the development of potential drug-drug interactions and adverse events.

In the previous chapters, specific treatment recommendations are given for the use of both psychotherapy and pharmacotherapy in the major psychiatric disorders. Most of these strategies will also apply to the older adult. However, as with any specific population, there are special considerations and conditions that arise. This chapter addresses some of these clinical concerns as they impact on the older adult. Treatment guidelines are offered on the following: psychotherapeutic considerations; pharmacologic interventions; affective disorders; late onset psychosis; anxiety disorders; psychiatric illness and stroke; and psychiatric illness and cardiac disease.

PSYCHOTHERAPEUTIC CONSIDERATIONS IN THE OLDER ADULT

There are both social and cultural aspects of aging that impact us all and need to be considered when one is working with the older adult. Also, society and values continue to change rapidly in the United States, challenging the security of many older adults. The percentage of the population over 65 has increased from 4 percent in 1900 to about 12 percent currently. In addition, the average life expectancy is now over 80 years of age (Heinz, 1984). Certain fears accompany growing old, but these fears are often magnified when compared to the reality of what older Americans experience. In a survey, Heinz (1984) found that specific fears such as running out of funds to live, poor health, loneliness, and lack of medical care are anticipated by those under age 65, two to five times more than actually are reported by the elderly.

The clinician should be familiar with these distortions when evaluating elderly patients, or they may become barriers to the establishment of a therapeutic alliance. The psychiatric evaluation should also explore important late-life milestones: retirement, loss of social status, fixed financial resources, menopause, reduced sexual potency, children leaving home, becoming a grandparent, death of an adult child, death of friends, the diagnosis of irreversible illness, and other events. These are some of the developmental tasks of late life that when poorly mastered can either present as or aggravate a psychiatric illness. A clinician treating an older adult may use psychotherapeutic techniques similar to those used with a younger patient, but a working knowledge of later-life issues is needed.

Other age-related concerns in psychotherapy are altered transference and countertransference. A reverse transference (Grunes, 1987) can occur where the clinician, perhaps 30 years younger than the patient, becomes the child and the patient the parent in the relationship. The common notion that "one is too old to change" needs to be addressed by both the clinician working with the older adult and the patient. All studies have shown that psychotherapeutic interventions are effective in the elderly. What studies failed to find, however, was an advantage of one psychotherapeutic technique over another.

Thompson and colleagues (1987) studied 91 older subjects with major depression, randomizing them into four treatment groups: cognitive therapy, behavioral therapy, brief psychodynamic therapy, and waiting list control. All therapeutic approaches showed similar efficacy at the end of 16 to 20 individual therapy sessions. The mean age of patients was 67. At two years follow-up, 77% of those who were recovered by the end of treatment remained well. In this study, 52% responded completely to psychotherapy. Other studies in the elderly show similar efficacy for psychotherapy in major depression, but fail to find a significant difference between cognitive, behavioral, or brief dynamic approaches (Marman et al., 1989). Some modification for cognitive therapy in the elderly has been suggested (Thompson et al., 1986). Group therapies also have been effective interventions in the elderly (Leszcz, 1987).

GUIDELINES FOR PSYCHOTHERAPEUTIC CONSIDERATIONS IN THE OLDER ADULT

1. **Clinicians need to familiarize themselves with late life developmental issues and late-life stressors.**
   Although the clinician may not have experienced these life milestones, the basic principles of psychotherapy still apply (that is, one does not have to experience a rape to help a victim overcome the fears and anguish of the trauma).
2. **Clinicians need to examine their own fears and stereotypes, concerning aging, to avoid these becoming barriers to the establishment of a therapeutic relationship with an older adult.**
   Many older adults still approach psychiatric treatment with significant stigma and feelings of personal inadequacy.
3. **Transference issues are at times different for clinicians working with the elderly.**
   Parent and child transference may occur with the clinician assuming the role of the child in the relationship. Clinicians need to be aware of unresolved issues with their own parents in order to recognize these influences in their therapeutic work with the older adult.
4. **All therapeutic interventions, whether based on cognitive, interpersonal, behavioral, or psychodynamic approaches, can effect change in the older adult.**
   Several controlled studies have failed to demonstrate the superiority of any one approach over another.
5. **Specific goals of therapy, whether interpersonal, intrapsychic, social, or behavioral, should be made explicit in the beginning of treatment.**
   Vague goals of personality change are less effective in establishing a therapeutic alliance and accomplishing subsequent symptom relief.
6. **Goals of therapy should reflect the individual's unique circumstances.**
   These would include the extent of the distress, the reality of the daily life situation, and the possibility of limited life expectancy (e.g., past losses in a 60-year-old may be mourned, but past ac-

complishments may still be a source of life-appreciation and self-esteem).

SPECIFIC PHARMACOLOGIC CONSIDERATIONS IN THE OLDER ADULT

Physiological changes in aging often have a direct impact on the pharmacologic management of illness in the elderly. The physiology of aging has been well studied and outlined in the work of Shock and colleagues (1984), *Normal Human Aging: The Baltimore Longitudinal Study of Aging.* The specific changes in the human body that impact pharmacologic treatment are varied.

Although there are age-related changes in the digestive system, the absorption of pharmaceuticals usually remains adequate and rarely poses a clinical problem. Changes in the liver and kidney do, however, alter the pharmacokinetics of many drugs. With age, there is progressive loss of renal mass and renal blood flow. As the kidney's filtration capacity decreases, reflected by a reduced creatinine clearance, drugs and metabolites that are primarily excreted by this route show a proportional increase in half-life. Reduced doses are necessary to avoid excessive drug levels and subsequent adverse effects. One psychoactive medication that is primarily excreted by the kidneys is lithium carbonate. Lithium can be used in the elderly if serum levels are judiciously monitored. Therapeutic lithium serum levels may be reached at one-fourth to one-half of the usual adult dose. All other commonly used psychoactive agents are at least partially excreted in the biliary system, which tends to minimize but not eliminate the effect of decreasing renal function on the drug's serum level.

The majority of psychoactive drugs are either transformed or metabolized in the liver. The functional activity of the liver's critical metabolic enzyme systems is not significantly affected by age. Many compounds, including most anticonvulsants and barbiturates, directly induce these enzyme systems. Alcohol use and smoking also stimulate hepatic metabolism. In one large study, age accounted for only 3 percent of the variability of hepatic drug clearance between subjects (Vestal et al., 1975). This finding is consistent with clinical experience. In our Geropsychiatry Clinic, we have seen individuals in their seventies reach therapeutic nortriptyline serum levels at daily doses that have ranged from 10 mg to 150 mg. Our clinic staff have accepted the fact that we are not able to predict a patient's ability to hepatically metabolize a drug on the basis of physical appearance or exam (Jenike, 1982).

Other physiological changes that affect pharmacokinetics are decreasing albumin, decreasing free water, and increasing total body fat with age. Most psychoactive drugs, with the exception of lithium and venlafaxine, are highly protein-bound (greater than 90 percent). As available protein binding sites decrease with age, there is potential for increased levels of free drug reaching the target organ, especially if multiple medications are being taken. Highly lipophilic agents, such as the longer acting benzodiazepines, demonstrate a progressively prolonged half-life with age, in part due to the increase in body fat (Greenblatt, Sellers, & Shader, 1982). The net clinical impact of these changes is that the elderly usually require lower doses and are more likely to experience both the common and the more unusual side effects of psychoactive drugs.

Lastly, there are issues of receptor sensitivity and plasticity. Studies with receptor specific agents such as beta-blockers (Propranolol) show the older adult having a blunted clinical response to receptor blockade (Vestal, Wood, & Shaud, 1979). Neuronal plasticity, an ability of the neuron to alter receptor sensitivity or density, also decreases with age (Frolkis et al., 1984). On the other hand, the aged brain is clearly more sensitive to the sedative property of any pharmacologic agent and more sensitive to the confusional effect of agents with anticholinergic properties. These changes allow us to understand why individuals may have tolerated a tricyclic well into their forties but find the same agent causing frank delirium in their sixties.

GUIDELINES FOR PSYCHOPHARMACOLOGIC TREATMENT OF THE ELDERLY

1. **For any psychoactive drug, start with a dose that is around one-half of the usual adult starting dose.**
   Monitor the patient closely for excessive sedation, onset of confusion, or emergence of toxicity from other medications concurrently prescribed.
2. **Remember that some elderly will require the full adult dose to achieve clinical efficacy.**

This is most common with the antidepressants. Metabolic activity of the hepatic enzyme systems usually cannot be determined from physical appearance or exam.

3. **Utilize serum levels whenever available.**
For example, some elderly will show significant side effects with relatively low doses of antidepressants. They may either not tolerate the particular drug or experience a high serum level with a relatively low dose. Only a serum drug level would answer the question.
4. **Avoid the use of long half-life drugs in the older adult (e.g., diazepam, chlordiazepoxide, flurazepam, and fluoxetine).**
Drugs with long half-lives usually demonstrate an even longer serum half-life as people age. In many older adults, this leads to an increased incidence of elevated serum levels and adverse events.
5. **The ability to tolerate an anticholinergic load decreases with age.**
Review all drugs the patient may be taking to evaluate anticholinergic load (for example, diphenhydramine, scopolamine patches, metoclopramide, and over-the-counter cold and sleep preparations). Avoid the use of highly anticholinergic drugs if alternatives are available (for example, amitriptyline, doxepin, clomipramine, chlorpromazine, and thioridazine). If confusion develops, stop all agents immediately and reevaluate the medication regime.

COMMON PSYCHIATRIC DISORDERS IN THE OLDER ADULT

Major depression is one of the most common psychiatric illnesses in late life, with an incidence approaching 15% of older community residents (NIH Consensus Conference, 1992). Despite its frequency, it remains relatively underdiagnosed and undertreated in this population. There are several likely reasons for this. Since the elderly often suffer from several chronic medical conditions, many individuals view depression as being "natural" or "to be expected." These attitudes have been seen by us even in medical students. Another reason for undertreatment is that major depression is more difficult to diagnose in older adults. Symptoms of major depression appearing for the first time in someone aged 60 require a thorough physical examination by someone familiar with medical causes of depression-like symptoms. Major depression often presents with different symptomatology in the older adult. Two specific symptom presentations have been named masked depression and pseudodementia. In masked depression, the patient presents primarily with somatic complaints. A typical case could be an older adult complaining of fatigue, pain in various areas, and not feeling well, but not endorsing the psychological symptoms usually associated with depression (Keilholz, 1973).

Pseudodementia is a term applied to a major depression in which the presentation partially mimics that of a primary dementia. General apathy, slowed mentation, concentration impairment, and lack of emotional responsivity are characteristic of pseudodementia. The psychological symptoms of overt sadness, tearfulness, and despair may be minimal or even absent (Caine, 1981). This presentation is similar to and can be mistaken for dementia.

To help arrive at the appropriate diagnosis, the clinician may need to schedule additional time with the patient and family. The patient's prior history, family history for affective disorder, and time course of onset need to be explored. Patient effort during the mental status exam should also be considered, along with the results of a complete medical evaluation. In these cases, imaging studies of the brain, such as Computerized Tomography (CT) or Magnetic Resonance Imaging (MRI), and functional brain studies, such as Electroencephalography (EEG), or Single Photon Computerized Electron Tomography (SPECT), may help in the diagnosis. The Yesavage Geriatric Rating Scale is a simple psychometric instrument that may help identify the depressed older adult even with the presence of significant physical illness (Yesavage et al., 1983).

If doubt about the diagnosis remains, treatment for depression should be attempted to prevent the patient and the family from needlessly suffering in the face of a reversible condition. Studies demonstrate that major depression in the older adult responds to appropriate treatment as well as in younger age cohorts (Hinrichsen, 1992; Stoudemire et al., 1993).

The symptoms of mania in manic-depressive illness may also differ in late life. Euphoria and grandiosity become less common and seem to be replaced by irritability and aggressiveness. Some individuals, as they age, may also become intolerant of lithium carbonate and begin displaying signs of neurotoxicity, even with therapeutic serum levels.

For these patients, valproic acid or carbomazepine should be considered as alternate maintenance agents.

GUIDELINES FOR TREATMENT OF DEPRESSION IN THE OLDER ADULT

1. **In the older adult presenting with new symptoms of depression or symptoms of depression and dementia, a complete medical evaluation is indicated.**
   The family should be interviewed with regards to behavior and symptoms. Confounding factors such as concurrent nonpsychiatric medication, concurrent medical illness, or other coexisting psychiatric conditions should be systematically explored for their contribution to the depressive symptoms.
2. **Major depression may present with atypical symptoms in the older adult.**
   Masked depression and pseudodementia are recognized forms of major depression that are most often seen in the elderly.
3. **Initiate pharmacotherapy with the cautions outlined earlier in the chapter.**
   Nortriptyline is the most widely used tricyclic antidepressant in the elderly. The availability of serum levels and the existence of a defined therapeutic window allow the clinician to clearly arrive at a therapeutic dose. The newer antidepressants such as the selective serotonin re-uptake inhibitors, bupropion, venlafaxine, and trazadone have the general advantage of fewer side effects and safety in overdose. The few studies of these agents in the elderly report comparable efficacy when compared to the tricyclics. Dosing requirements of the newer agents are less clear in the medically ill or elderly.
4. **Initiate psychotherapy with pharmacotherapy.**
   For individuals hesitant to take medication, psychotherapy has been shown effective in major depression unless melancholic features are present.
5. **If treatment is ineffective, reconsider the possibility of an occult medical condition either causing or interfering with treatment.**
   Reexamine the symptoms as to the presence of any psychotic material. A depression with psychotic symptoms generally requires an antipsychotic with the antidepressant or electroconvulsive therapy for successful treatment.

6. **Some older adults may respond only to electroconvulsive therapy.**
   Perhaps this reflects changes in neuronal plasticity or sensitivity in aging. Even if this is the case, attempts at other interventions should continue. Relapse after a course of electroconvulsive therapy is not an uncommon problem.
7. **Maintenance treatment should continue for at least six months to one year after the remission of symptoms.**
   If the individual is known to have a recurrent problem with depression, maintenance treatment may be continued indefinitely.

LATE ONSET PSYCHOSIS (PARAPHRENIAS)

Kraepelin first introduced the concept of "paraphrenia" in 1909. He described the syndrome as the presence of psychotic symptoms, usually paranoid delusions and occasionally hallucinations, beginning in middle to late life. He wanted to separate this from schizophrenia because of the later age of onset and the more intact personality structure and functional ability of this patient group.

Today, little more is known about paraphrenia outside of Kraepelin's original observations. It has been estimated that 10% of psychiatric admissions for patients over 60 are for late-onset psychosis (Leuchter & Spar, 1985). The disorder occurs in women much more frequently than in men, and presents mainly with paranoid delusions. There is a spectrum of severity, however, with some patients presenting with hallucinations and a formal thought disorder (Post, 1966).

Studies point to several risk factors in these patients. The incidence of a suspicious or schizotypal premorbid personality, loss of visual or auditory acuity, social isolation, and nonspecific brain injury are all greater in patients with late-onset psychosis (Pearlson & Robins, 1988).

GUIDELINES FOR TREATMENT OF LATE-ONSET PSYCHOSIS

1. **As with any significant mental status change in older adults, the new onset of psychotic symptoms warrants a complete medical evaluation.**

Medications, aphasic syndromes, epileptic states, paraneoplastic syndromes, all can produce an altered mental status appearing similar to a functional psychosis.

2. **Attempt to establish a therapeutic alliance with the patient.** This may be difficult because of the presence of paranoia, but it is vital for longitudinal treatment.
3. **Antipsychotics are often effective in reducing the paranoia and may also lead to complete remission of symptoms.** In general, lower doses of antipsychotics are required when compared to the treatment of early-onset schizophrenia.
4. **Consider appropriate referrals if hearing or visual impairments are felt to be contributing factors.** Hearing and visual impairment have been linked to the development of suspicion and even paranoia in many individuals, not only the elderly.
5. **Compliance with medications is the most difficult problem encountered in this population.** Very low doses of decanoate preparations (for example, fluphenazine decanoate 12.5 mg per month) can be an effective approach.

ANXIETY DISORDERS IN THE OLDER ADULT

Anxiety disorders in the older adult have not been well studied. It would be uncommon for panic disorder or obsessive-compulsive disorder to first appear in the older adult. Generalized anxiety disorder may be common but is mostly a lifelong condition. The abrupt onset of a significant anxiety state in the older adult needs to be carefully explored while one remains alert to the various possible medical and psychological precipitants. Persistent anxiety states have been reported following traumatic events such as a cardiac arrest or other near-death experiences.

GUIDELINES FOR TREATMENT OF ANXIETY DISORDERS IN THE OLDER ADULT

1. **The new onset of significant anxiety in the older adult needs to be carefully evaluated.**

Is it a psychologic reaction to some event or fear? Is it medication-induced? Is it secondary to a new illness (i.e., hyperthyroidism)? Is it an agitated depression?

2. **If the symptoms prove to be functional anxiety, psychotherapeutic interventions should be attempted before medications.**
3. **Although benzodiazepines are very effective anxiolytics, the older adult is at much higher risk for dizziness, daytime sedation, incoordination, and falling from these agents.** Actual cognitive impairment, especially in short-term memory, acute confusional states, and paradoxical disinhibition are not uncommon adverse events seen with benzodiazepine use in the elderly. If a benzodiazepine is used, attempt a time-limited course of treatment. Avoid the very potent agents such as alprazolam and the long half-life agents such as diazepam. Consider the use of buspirone as it has been shown to lack significant side effects in the elderly (Goldberg, 1994). Antidepressants have also shown efficacy in anxiety disorders and do present an alternative pharmacologic approach.

PSYCHIATRIC ILLNESS AND STROKE

Cerebrovascular accidents occur in over 300,000 individuals in the United States annually (Wolf et al., 1977). In addition, stroke is the third leading cause of mortality and morbidity, behind only heart disease and cancer. There are many neuropsychiatric sequelae to brain injury, depending upon the size and location of the lesion. Three of the most common problems presented to the psychiatrist are (1) cognitive impairment, (2) personality and behavior changes, and (3) post-stroke depression (PSD).

The cognitive impairment seen following stroke necessarily reflects the specific areas of the brain that have been injured. Many patients subsequently exhibit what has been called "the catastrophic reaction," a symptom also seen in patients with primary degenerative dementia. Basically, some seemingly minor event or disagreement is met with an exaggerated emotional outburst, often with uncharacteristic anger, cursing, and even aggression. A clinical scenario would be a grandfather taking out the garbage and accidentally dropping an item. He subsequently flies into a rage shouting and throwing the garbage around the room. Treatment with serotonergic antidepressants and buspirone, which also enhances serotonin neurotransmission, may ameliorate this reaction (Herrmann & Eryavec, 1993). Controlled studies in this area with the newer serotonergic agents are needed.

Early family intervention is needed. *The 36-Hour Day* (Mace & Rabins, 1991) is a very useful tool in helping family members understand the consequences of brain injury and help diffuse the anger that is often generated and directed at the patient with behavioral problems.

Personality changes occur, especially in frontal or tempo-parietal area lesions. These commonly manifest themselves as socially inappropriate behavior, social withdrawal, mood swings, and impulse control problems. Studies comparing various interventions are almost nonexistent. In our experience, pharmacotherapy may improve mood swings and impulsivity, but does little to affect other aspects of altered personality. Psychotherapeutic support and education for the caregivers or family are appropriate interventions and may not only reduce stress in the family but also facilitate recovery after stroke (Chiverton & Caine, 1989; Lansky, 1984).

Although Kraepelin and Bleuler both noted mood changes after stroke, it was Post (1962) who suggested the existence of a causal link between stroke and depression. When PSD was systematically compared to DSM-III defined Major Depression, the symptom profiles of both were found to be identical (Lipsey et al., 1986). Other studies found that depressive symptoms occurred in over half of patients with left hemisphere injury, but only slightly over 10 percent of those with a right hemisphere lesion (Robinson et al., 1984). More recent studies suggest that the highest incidence of depressive syndromes occurs from specific lesions in the left anterior cortex and the left basal ganglion (Eastwood et al., 1989; Starkstein et al., 1988). Controlled studies using nortriptyline and trazadone show clear efficacy of antidepressants in the treatment of PSD (Lipsey et al., 1984; Reding, Orto, & Winter, 1986).

GUIDELINES FOR TREATMENT OF PSYCHIATRIC ILLNESS AND STROKE

1. **Many neuropsychiatric problems seen in brain injury often require a multifaceted treatment approach.**

Global recovery may be facilitated by early family inclusion in the education and the post-stroke rehabilitation effort. Respite care, day care, and other community resources may need to be explored in certain situations.

2. **Caregivers and families should be encouraged to read *The 36-Hour Day* (Mace & Rabins, 1991) and urged to participate in local support groups.**
   Many day-to-day management and survival techniques for families are taught by other caregivers who find themselves in similar life circumstances.
3. **Anger outbursts, impulsivity, and mood lability subsequent to brain injury may be improved by various pharmacologic interventions.**
   Consider empiric trials of serotonergic antidepressants, buspirone, beta-blockers, and anticonvulsants. Trials of antipsychotic agents and benzodiazepines may also be worthwhile if the other approaches fail, but they are generally less efficacious.
4. **Be alert for the development of post-stroke depression in a patient.**
   Lesions affecting the left anterior cortex and the left basil ganglia may result in an incidence of depressive syndromes of over 80 percent. This depression should be treated aggressively with antidepressants with the expectation of a full recovery.
5. **Electroconvulsive therapy has been found to be effective in PSD and can be considered if other interventions fail.**

PSYCHIATRIC ILLNESS AND CARDIAC DISEASE

Although the heart has been the historical seat of love and emotion, modern neuroscience disavows a link. Heart disease however is the most frequent cause of death in the United States. The often quoted Epidemiologic Catchment Area Survey (Eaton et al., 1984) found that individuals over 55 with a mood disorder had a fourfold higher mortality rate than expected. Over half these deaths were from coronary artery disease or stroke. How do depression and coronary artery disease together lead to increased morality? Compliance with treatment and life-style change may be one link (Blumenthal et al., 1982). The inherent symptoms of depression mitigate against the goals of most cardiac rehabilitation regimes. Another link may be the physiologic effects of simple stress. Mental stress, which occurs in depression, has been shown to induce cardiac ischemia (Rozanski et al., 1988).

The prevalence of minor and major depression has been reported to be as high as 45 percent in individuals with a recent myocardial infarction (Schleifer et al., 1989). The presence of depression is also a risk factor for major cardiac events (Carney et al., 1988). Although some of the minor depression after myocardial infarct may be a clear psychological reaction to a serious life event, the relationship of depression to increased morbidity and mortality should not be minimized.

Clinicians can be hesitant in treating cardiac patients with antidepressants. Most often, an agent can be safely used when the clinician is familiar with the drug's cardiac properties and the patient's cardiac disease. A comprehensive discussion of the safety of various antidepressants in the cardiac patient is beyond the scope of this chapter, but can be found in *Psychiatric Care of the Medical Patient* (Stoudemire, Fogel, et al., 1993).

GUIDELINES FOR TREATMENT OF PSYCHIATRIC ILLNESS AND CARDIAC DISEASE

1. **The presence of depression is associated with much higher morbidity and mortality in individuals with coronary artery disease.**
   Given the high prevalence of depression following myocardial infarction or coronary artery bypass surgery, it is imperative that the clinician be alert for this complication and initiate treatment in a timely manner.
2. **Treatment of depression in the cardiac patient should be aggressive.**
   Psychotherapeutic and pharmacologic interventions show similar efficacy in this population as in the treatment of the noncardiac patient.
3. **Psychotherapeutic approaches should address lifestyle and other behaviors that increase the risk for future coronary events (for example, diet, exercise, smoking, obesity, and stress).**

Much has been written and debated about the "Type A" personality and coronary artery disease. Depression, however, clearly increases mortality and morbidity irrespective of personality style.

4. **Orthostatic hypotension is often a problem seen with the use of antidepressants in patients with cardiac disease.**
   This is a theoretically interesting although currently unexplained observation. Studies have shown that patients with depression and cardiac disease have more problems with orthostatic hypotension than cardiac patients without depression.
5. **The clinician should be familiar with the patient's cardiac condition and the cardiac profile of the antidepressant before prescribing.**
   In most cases, an antidepressant can be found that is safe and effective.
6. **Electroconvulsive therapy remains a viable option for individuals either unusually intolerant of or nonresponsive to antidepressants or psychotherapy.**

References

Alden, L. (1989). Short-term structured treatment for avoidant personality disorder. *Journal of Consulting and Clinical Psychology, 57*, 756–764.

American Psychiatric Association. (1980). Guidelines for psychiatrists in consultation, supervisory, or collaborating relationships with nonmedical therapists. *American Journal of Psychiatry, 137*, 1489–1491.

American Psychiatric Association. (1993). Practice guideline for eating disorders. *American Journal of Psychiatry, 150*: 2, 212–227.

Anderson, C., Reiss, D., & Hogarty, G. (1986). *Schizophrenia and the family*. New York: Guilford.

Applebaum, P. (1991). General guidelines for psychiatrists who prescribe medication for patients treated by nonmedical psychotherapists. *Hospital and Community Psychiatry, 42*, 281–282.

Applebaum, P., & Guthiel, T. (1991). *Clinical handbook of psychiatry and the law* (2nd ed.) Baltimore: Williams & Wilkins.

Appleby, L., Pesai, P. N., Luchins, D. J., et al. (1993). Length of stay and recidivism in schizophrenia: A study of public psychiatric hospital patients. *American Journal of Psychiatry, 150*, 72–76.

Awad, G. (1993). Subjective response to neuroleptics in schizophrenia. *Schizophrenia Bulletin, 19*, 609–618.

Baer, L., & Jenike, M. (1992). Personality disorders in obsessive compulsive disorder. *Psychiatric Clinics in North America, 15*, 803–812.

Barlow, D., & Waddell, M. (1985). Agoraphobia. In D. Barlow (Ed.), *Clinical handbook of psychological disorders: A step-by-step treatment manual.* New York: Guilford.

Beaudry, P. (1991). Generalized anxiety disorder. In B. Beitman & G. Klerman (Eds.), *Integrating pharmacotherapy and psychotherapy*. Washington, DC: American Psychiatric Press, 211–230.

Beavers, R. (1985). *Successful marriage: A family systems approach to couple therapy*. New York: Norton.

Beavers, R., Hampson, R. (1990). *Successful families: Assessment and intervention.* New York: Norton.

Beck, A., Freeman, A., & Associates (1990). *Cognitive therapy of the personality disorders.* New York: Guilford.

Beck, A., Rush, A., Shaw, B., & Emery, G. (1979). *Cognitive therapy of depression.* New York: Guilford.

Beitman, B. (1991). Medication during psychotherapy: Case studies of the reciprocal relationship between psychotherapy process and medication use. In B. Beitman & G. Klerman (Eds.), *Integrating pharmacotherapy and psychotherapy.* Washington, DC: American Psychiatric Press, 21–44.

Beitman, B. (1993a). Combined treatments. In J. Oldham, M. Riba, & A. Tasman (Eds.), *American psychiatric press review of psychiatry, Volume 12.* Washington, DC: American Psychiatric Press, 517–519.

Beitman, B. (1993b). Pharmacotherapy and the stages of psychotherapeutic change. In J. Oldham, M. Riba, & A. Tasman (Eds.), *American psychiatric press review of psychiatry, volume 12.* Washington, DC: American Psychiatric Press, 521–540.

Beitman, B. & Klerman, G. (Eds.) (1991). *Integrating pharmacotherapy and psychotherapy.* Washington, DC: American Psychiatric Press.

Beitman, B. & Mooney, J. (1991). Exposure and desensitization as common change process in pharmacotherapy and psychotherapy. In B. Beitman & G. Klerman (Eds.), *Integrating pharmacotherapy and psychotherapy.* Washington, DC: American Psychiatric Press. 435–446.

Benjamin, L. (1993). *Interpersonal diagnosis and treatment of personality disorders.* New York: Guilford.

Bennett, M. (1993). View from the bridge: Reflections of a recovering staff model HMO psychiatrist. *Psychiatric Quarterly, 64,* 45–75.

Beutler, L. & Clarkin, J. (1990). *Systemic treatment selection: Toward targeted therapist interventions.* New York: Brunner/Mazel.

Bills, L. J., & Kreisler, K. (1993). Treatment of flashbacks with naltrexone. Letters to the Editor. *American Journal of Psychiatry, 150,* 1430.

Bisbee, C. (1991). *Educating patients and families about mental illness: A practical guide.* Gaithersburg, MD: Aspen Publishers.

Blackwell, B. (1976). Treatment adherence. *British Journal of Psychiatry, 129,* 513–531.

Blackwell, B., & Schmidt, G. (1992). The educational implications of managed mental health care. *Hospital and Community Psychiatry, 43,* 962–964.

Blumenthal, J., Williams, R., Wallace, A., et al. (1982). Physiological and psychological variables predict compliance to prescribed exercise therapy in patients recovering from myocardial infarction. *Psychosomatic Medicine, 44,* 519–527.

Bohn, J., & Jefferson, J. (1992). *Lithium and manic depression: A guide* (Rev. Ed.) Madison, WI: Dean Foundation.

Breier, A., & Strauss, J. (1983). Self-control in psychotic disorders. *Archives of General Psychiatry, 40,* 1141–1145.

Brock, D. (1993). Medication groups. In A. Alonzo & H. Sweller (Eds.), *Group therapy in clinical practice.* Washington, DC: American Psychiatric Press, 155–169.

Brook, D. (1993). Group psychotherapy with anxiety and mood disorders. In H. Kaplan & B. Sadock (Eds.), *Comprehensive group psychotherapy* (3rd Ed). Baltimore: Williams & Wilkins, 374–393.

Brotman, A. W. (1994). What works in the treatment of anorexia nervosa? *The Harvard mental health letter, 10* (7), 8.

Brown, R., & Lewinsohn, P. (1984). A psychoeducational approach to the treatment of depression: Comparison of group, individual, and minimal contact procedures. *Journal of Consulting and Clinical Psychology*, *52*, 774–783.

Budman, S. (1992). Models of brief individual and group psychotherapy. In J. Feldman & R. Fitzpatrick (Eds.), *Managed mental health care.* Washington, DC: American Psychiatric Press, 231–247.

Busch, F., & Gould, E. (1993). Treatment by a psychotherapist and psychopharmacologist: Transference and countertransference issues. *Hospital and Community Psychiatry*, *44*, 772–774.

Butler, G. (1989). Phobia disorders. In K. Hawton, P. Salkovskis, J. Kirk, & D. Clark (Eds.), *Cognitive behavior therapy for psychiatric problems: A practical guide.* Oxford: Oxford University Press, 97–128.

Caine, E. (1981). Pseudodementia. *Archives of General Psychiatry*, *38*, 1359–1364.

Carney, R., Rich, M., Freedland, K., et al. (1988). Major depressive disorder predicts cardiac events in patients with coronary artery disease. *Psychosomatic Medicine*, *50*, 627–633.

Chiles, J., Carlin, A., Benjamin, G., & Beitman, B. (1991). A physician, a nonmedical psychotherapist and a patient: The pharmacotherapy-psychotherapy triangle. In B. Beitman & G. Klerman (Eds.), *Integrating pharmacotherapy and psychotherapy.* Washington, DC: American Psychiatric Press, 105–118.

Chiverton, P., & Caine, E. (1989). Education to assist spouses in coping with Alzheimer's Disease. *Journal of the American Geriatric Society*, *37*, 593–598.

Clark, D. (1989). Anxiety states: Panic and generalized anxiety. In K. Hawton, P Salkovskis, J. Kirk, & D. Clark (Eds.), *Cognitive behavior therapy for psychiatric problems: A practical guide.* Oxford: Oxford University Press, 52–96.

Coccaro, F., & Kavoussi, R. (1991). Biological and pharmacological aspects of borderline personality disorder. *Hospital and Community Psychiatry*, *42*, 1029–1033.

Cochran, S. (1984). Preventing medical noncompliance in the outpatient treatment of bipolar affective disorders. *Journal of Consulting and Clinical Psychology*, *52* (5), 873–878.

Cowdry, R. W., & Gardner, D. L. (1988). Pharmacotherapy of borderline personality disorder. *Archives of General Psychiatry*, *45*, 111–119.

Cowley, D., & Roy-Burne, P. (1988). Panic disorders: Psychological aspects. *Psychiatric Annals*, *18*, 465–467.

Craske, M., & Waikar, S. (1994). Panic disorder. In M. Hersen & R. Ammerman (Eds.), *Handbook of prescribing of prescriptive treatments for adults.* New York: Plenum, 135–156.

Cummings, M. A., Haviland, M. G., Wareham, J. G., et al. (1993). A prospective clinical evaluation of an equation to predict daily lithium dose. *Journal of Clinical Psychiatry*, *54*, 55–58.

Davenport, Y., Ebert, M., Adland, M., & Goodwin, F. (1977). Couples group therapy as an adjunct to lithium maintenance of the manic patient. *American Journal of Orthopsychiatry*, *47*, 495–502.

Davis, J., Kane, J., Marder, S., et al. (1993). Dose response of prophylactic antipsychotics. *Journal of Clinical Psychiatry*, *54*, 2(suppl).

Dekle, D., & Christensen, L. (1990). Medication management. *Hospital and Community Psychiatry*, *41*, 96–97.

Deltito, J., & Stam, M. (1989). Pharmacological treatment of avoidant personality disorder. *Comprehensive Psychiatry*, *30*, 498–504.

Diamond, R., & Little, M. (1984). Utilization of patient expertise in medication groups. *Psychiatric Quarterly, 56,* 13–19.

Docherty, J. (1988). Managing compliance problems in psychopharmacology. In F. Flack (Ed.), *Psychobiology and psychopharmacology, Volume 2.* New York: Norton, 12–31.

Doherty, W., & Baird, M. (1983). *Family therapy and family medicine.* New York: Guilford.

Eastwood, M., Rifat, S., Nobbs, H., et al. (1989). Mood disorder following cerebrovascular accident. *British Journal of Psychiatry, 154,* 195–200.

Eaton, W., Regier, D., Locke, B., et al. (1984). The epidemiologic catchment area program of the national institute of mental health. *Public Health Report, 96,* 319–325.

Eckman, T., & Liberman, R. (1990a). Teaching medication management skills to schizophrenic patients. *Journal of Clinical Psychopharmacology, 10,* 33–38.

Eckman, T., & Liberman, R. (1990b). A large-scale field test of medication management skills training program for people with schizophrenia. *Psychosocial Rehabilitation Journal, 13,* 31–35.

Eckman, T., Liberman, R., Phipps, C., & Blair, K. (1990). Teaching medication management skills to schizophrenic patients. *Journal of Classical Psychopharmacology, 10,* 33–38.

Elkin, I. (1994). The NIMH treatment of depression collaborative research program: Where we began and where we are. In A. Bergin & S. Garfield (Eds.), *Handbook of psychotherapy and behavior change, 4th ed.* New York: Wiley, 114–139.

Elkin, I., Shea, M., Watkins, J., et al. (1989). National Institute of Mental Health treatment of depression collaborative research program: General effectiveness of treatments. *Archives of General Psychiatry, 46,* 971–992.

Elkin, I., Shea, M., Watkins, J., et al. (1989). NIMH treatment of depression collaborative research, Program I: General effectiveness of treatments. *Archives of General Psychiatry, 46,* 971–982.

Fallon, I., & Liberman, R. (1983). Behavioral family interventions in the management of chronic schizophrenia. In W. McFarlane (Ed.), *Family therapy in schizophrenia.* New York: Guilford, 117–140.

Fava, M., & Kaji, J. (1994). Continuation and maintenance treatments of major depressive disorder. *Psychiatric Annals, 24,* 281–290.

Fawcett, J., Epstein, P., Fiester, S. J., et al. (1987). Clinical management–imipramine/placebo administration manual: NIMH Treatment of Depression Collaborative Research Program. *Pharmacology Bulletin, 23,* 309–324.

Fawcett, J. (1994). Some provocative thoughts about continuation and maintenance therapy. *Psychiatric Annals, 24,* 279–280.

Fawcett, J. (1995). Compliance: Definitions and key issues. *Journal of Clinical Psychiatry, 56* (suppl.1), 4–8.

Feldman, J., & Fitzpatrick, R. (Eds.), (1992). *Managed mental health care: Administrative and clinical issues.* Washington, DC: American Psychiatric Press.

Feldman, L. (1992). *Integrating individual and family therapy.* New York: Brunner/Mazel.

Frances, A., Clarkin, J., & Perry, S. (1984). *Differential therapeutics in psychiatry: The art and science of treatment selection.* New York: Brunner/Mazel.

Frank, E., Perel, J., Mallinger, A., et al. (1992). Relationship of pharmacologic compliance to long-term prophylaxis in recurrent depression. *Psychopharmacological Bulletin, 28,* 231–235.

Frank, E., Prien, R. F., Jarrett, D. B., et al. (1991). Conceptualization and rationale for consensus definitions of terms in major depressive disorder: Response, remission, recovery, relapse, and recurrence. *Archives of General Psychiatry, 48,* 851–855

Frolkis, V., Tanoin, S., Martynenko, O., et al. (1984). Aging of the neurons. In V. Frolkis (Ed.), *Physiology of cell aging*. Basel: Karger, 1–28.
Fuerst, M. (1994). Psychotherapy's role in treatment of bipolar disorder praised at First International Conference. *Psychiatric Times, 1* (33) August.
Gabbard, G.O. (1992). Comparative indications for brief and extended hospitalization. In A. Tasman & A. Riba (Eds.), *Review of psychiatry, Volume 11.* Washington, DC: American Psychiatric Press, 503–517.
Gelernter, C., Uhde, T., Cimbolic, P., et al. (1991). Cognitive-behavioral and pharmacological treatment of social phobia. *Archives General Psychiatry, 48,* 938–945.
Giles, T. (1993). *Managed mental health care: A guide for practitioners, employers, and hospital administrators.* Boston: Allyn & Bacon.
Glick, I., Clarkin, J., & Goldsmith, S. (1993). Combining medication with family psychotherapy. In J. Oldham, M. Riba & A. Tasman, (Eds.), *American psychiatric press review of psychiatry, Volume 12.* Washington, DC: American Psychiatric Press, 585–610.
Goldberg, R. (1994). The use of buspirone in geriatric patients. *Journal of Clinical Psychiatry Monograph, 12,* 31–35.
Goldstein, M. (1991). Schizophrenia and family therapy. In B. Beitman & G. Klerman (Eds.), *Integrating pharmacotherapy and psychotherapy.* Washington, DC: American Psychiatric Press, 291–310.
Gonnella, J. S., Louis, P. Z., Zeleznik, C., et al. (1990). The problem of late hospitalization: A quality and cost issue. *Academic Medicine, 65,* 314–319.
Goodwin, F. (1994). Psychiatry. *Journal of the American Medical Association, 271,* 1707–1708.
Goodwin, F., & Jamison, K. (1990). *Manic-depressive illness.* New York: Oxford University Press.
Gray, B. H., & Field, M. J. (1989). *Controlling costs and changing patient care: The role of utilization management.* Washington, DC: National Academy Press.
Greenblatt, D., Sellers, E., & Shader, R. (1982). Drug disposition in old age. *New England Journal of Medicine, 306,* 1081–1088.
Greist, J. (1992a). An integrated approach to treatment of obsessive compulsive disorder. *Journal of Clinical Psychiatry, 53* (4, suppl.) 38–41.
Greist, J. (1992b). *Obsessive compulsive disorder: A guide.* Madison, WI: Information Systems, Dean Foundation.
Greist, J., & Jefferson, J. (1992)., *Panic disorder and agoraphobia: A guide.* Madison, WI: Information Systems, Dean Foundation.
Group for the Advancement of Psychiatry. (1975). *Pharmacotherapy and psychotherapy: Paradoxes, problems and progress, Volume 93, Report #93.* New York: Mental Health Materials, Inc.
Grunes, J. (1987). The aged in psychotherapy: Psychodynamic contributions to the treatment process. In J. Sadavoy & M. Leszcz (Eds.), *Treating the elderly with psychotherapy: The scope for change in later life.* Madison, CT: International Universities Press.
Gunderson, J. (1988). Personality disorders. In A. Nicholi (Ed.), *The new Harvard guide to psychiatry.* Cambridge: Harvard University, 337–357.
Guscott, R., & Grof, P. (1991). The clinical meaning of refractory depression: A review for the clinician. *American Journal of Psychiatry, 148,* 695–704.
Heard, H., & Linehan, M. (1994). Dialectical behavior therapy: An integrative approach to the treatment of borderline personality disorder. *Journal of Psychotherapy Integration, 4,* 55–82.
Heimberg, R., & Liebowitz, M. (1992). A multi-center comparison of the efficacy of phenelzine and cognitive-behavioral group treatment for social phobia. Paper presented at the 12th National Conference, *Anxiety Disorders Association of America.* Houston, TX. April, 1992.

Heinz, J. (1984). *Aging America.* U.S. Senate Special Committee on Aging, Washington, DC: U.S. Government Printing Office.
Herrmann, N., & Eryavec, G. (1993). Buspirone in the management of agitation and aggression associated with dementia. *American Journal of Geriatric Psychiatry, 1,* 249–253.
Hersen, M., & Ammerman, R. (Eds.), (1994). *Handbook of prescriptive treatment for adults.* New York: Plenum.
Hinrichson, G. (1992). Recovery and relapse from major depressive disorder in the elderly. *American Journal of Psychiatry, 149,* 1575–1579.
Hoberman, H., & Lewisohn, P. (1990). Behavioral approaches to the treatment of unipolar depression. In T. Karasu (Ed.), *Treatments of psychiatric disorders.* Washington, DC: American Psychiatric Press, 1846–1862 Ref-2.
Hogarty, G. (1984). Depot neuroleptics: The relevance of psychosocial factors. *Journal of Clinical Psychiatry, 45,* 36–42.
Hogarty, G. (1993). Prevention of relapse in chronic schizophrenic patients. *Journal of Clinical Psychiatry, 53,* (3, suppl.) 18–23.
Hollon, S. D., DeRubeis, R. J., Evans, M. D., et al. (1992). Cognitive therapy and pharmacotherapy for depression: Singly and in combination. *Archives of General Psychiatry, 49,* 774–781.
Hollon, S. D., & Fawcett, J. (1995). Combined medication and psychotherapy. In G. Gabbard (Ed.), *Treatment of Psychiatric disorders* (2nd ed.). Washington, DC: American Psychiatric Press, 1221–1236.
Hooley, J., & Teasdale, J. (1989). Predictors of relapse in unipolar depression: Expressed emotion, marital distress, and perceived criticism. *Journal of Abnormal Psychology, 98,* 229–235.
Hyland, J. (1991). Integrating psychotherapy and pharmacotherapy. *Bulletin of the Menninger Clinic, 55,* 205–215.
Jamison, K. (1991). Manic-depressive illness: The overlooked need for psychotherapy. In B. Beitman & G. Klerman (Eds.), *Integrating pharmacotherapy and psychotherapy.* Washington, DC: American Psychiatric Press, 409–422.
Jamison, K. & Goodwin, F. (1983). Psychotherapeutic issues in bipolar illness. In L. Greenspoon (Ed.), *Psychiatric update: The American Psychiatric Association annual review, Volume 2.* Washington, DC: American Psychiatric Press, 319–337.
Jaques, E., & Clement, S. (1991). *Executive leadership: A practical guide to managing complexity.* Cambridge, MA: Blackwell Business.
Jefferson, J., & Greist, J. (1993). *Valproate and manic depression: A guide.* Madison, WI: Dean Foundation.
Jenike, M. (1982). Using sedative drugs in the elderly. *Drug Therapy, 12,* 186–190.
Jenike, M. (1991). Obsessive-compulsive disorder. In B. Beitman & G. Klerman, (Eds.), *Integrating pharmacotherapy and psychotherapy.* Washington, DC: American Psychiatric Press, 183–210.
Joyce, P. (1992). Prediction of treatment response. In E. Paykel (Ed.), *Handbook of affective disorders (2nd ed.).* New York: Guilford, 453–462.
Kahn, D. (1990). The psychotherapy of mania. *Psychiatric Clinics of North America, 13,* 229–240.
Kanas, N. (1993). Group psychotherapy with bipolar patients: A review and synthesis. *International Journal of Group Psychotherapy, 43,* 321–333.
Kanas, N. (1993). Group psychotherapy with schizophrenia. In H. Kaplan & B. Sadock (Eds.), *Comprehensive group psychotherapy, 3rd ed.* New York: Williams & Wilkins. (407–418).

Karasu, T (1982). Psychotherapy and pharmacotherapy: Toward an integrated model. *American Journal of Psychotherapy, 139*, 1102–1113.

Katz, P. (1986). The role of the psychotherapies in the practice of psychiatry. *Canadian Journal of Psychiatry, 31*, 458–465.

Kavanaugh, D. (1992). Recent developments in expressed emotion and schizophrenia. *British Journal of Psychiatry, 160*, 601–620.

Kavoussi, R., Liv. J., & Coccaro, E. (1994). An open trial of sertraline in personality disordered patients with impulsive aggression. *Journal of Clinical Psychiatry, 55*, 137–141.

Kay, J. (1991). The influence of the curriculum in psychiatry residency education. *Psychiatric Quarterly, 62*, 95–104.

Keck, P. E., McElroy, S. L., Tugrul, K. C., et al. (1993). Valproate loading in the treatment of acute mania. *Journal of Clinical Psychiatry, 54*, 305–308.

Keilholz, P. (Ed.) (1973). *Masked depression: An international symposium.* Berne, Switerland: Haus Huber Publisher.

Kelly, K. (1992). Parallel treatment: Therapy with one clinician and medication with another. *Hospital and Community Psychiatry, 43*, 778–780.

Kennedy, J. (1992). *Fundamentals of psychiatric treatment planning.* Washington, DC: American Psychiatric Press.

Kisch, J. (1991). The need for psychopharmacological collaboration in managed mental health care. In C. Austad & W. Berman (Eds.), *Psychotherapy in managed health care.* Washington, DC: American Psychological Association, 81–85.

Klerman, G. (1978). Long-term treatment of affective disorders. In M. Lipton, A. DiMascia & K. Killian (Eds.), *Psychopharmacology: A generation of progress.* New York: Rosen Press, 1303–1311.

Klerman, G. (1986). Medication and psychotherapy. In A. Bergin & S. Garfield (Eds.), *Handbook of psychotherapy and behavior change (3rd ed.).* New York: Wiley.

Klerman, G. (1990). The psychiatric patient's right to effective treatment: Implications of Osheroff v. Chestnut Lodge. *American Journal of Psychiatry, 147*, 409–413.

Koenigsberg, H. (1991). Borderline personality disorder. In B. Beitman & G. Klerman (Eds.), *Integrating pharmacotherapy and psychotherapy.* Washington, DC: American Psychiatric Press, 271–290.

Koenigsberg, H. (1993). Combining psychotherapy and pharmacotherapy in the treatment of borderline patients. In J. Oldham, M. Riba & A. Tasman (Eds.), *American psychiatric press review of psychiatry, Volume 12.* Washington, DC: American Psychiatric Press. 541–564.

Korpell, H. (1984). *A guide for families of psychiatric hospital patients.* Washington, DC: American Psychiatric Press.

Lansky, J. (1984). Family psychotherapy of the patient with chronic organic brain syndrome. *Psychiatric Annals, 14*, 2–17.

Lesser, I., & Friedmann, C. (1980). Beyond medication: Group therapy for the chronic psychiatric patient. *International Journal of Group Psychotherapy, 30*, 187–199.

Leszcz, M. (1987). Group psychotherapy with the elderly. In J. Sadavoy & M. Leszcz (Eds.), *Treating the elderly with psychotherapy: The scope for change in later life.* Madison, CT: International Universities Press.

Leuchter, A., & Spar, J. (1985). The late onset psychoses: Clinical and diagnostic features. *Journal of Nervous Mental Diseases, 173*, 488–494.

Lewis, J., & Blotcky, M. (1993). Living and learning with managed care. *Academic Psychiatry, 17*, 186–192.

Lewis, J., Sperry, L., & Carlson, J. (1993). *Health counseling.* Pacific Groves, CA: Brooks/Cole.

Lewisohn, P., Munoz, R., Youngren, M., et al. (1978). *Control your depression.* Englewood Cliffs, NJ: Prentice Hall.

Liberman, P. B., McPhetres, E. B., Elliott, B., et al. (1993). Dimensions and predictors of change during brief psychiatric hospitalization. *General Hospital Psychiatry, 15,* 316–324.

Liberman, R. (1986). *Social and independent living skills: Medication management module: Trainee's manual.* Los Angeles: Rehabilitation Research and Training Center in Mental Illness.

Liberman, R. (1988). *Social and independent living skills: Symptom management module: Trainer's manual.* Los Angeles: Rehabilitation Research and Training Center in Mental Illness.

Liberman, R., De Risi, W., & Meuser, K. (1989). *Social skills training for psychiatric patients.* New York: Pergamon.

Liebowitz, M., Schneier, F., Hollander, E., et al. (1991). Treatment of social phobia with drugs other than benzodiazepines. *Journal of Clinical Psychiatry, 52* (suppl.) 10–15.

Linehan, M. (1987). Dialectical behavior therapy: A cognitive behavioral approach to parasuicide. *Journal of Personality Disorders, 14,* 328–333.

Linehan, M., Armstrong, H., Suarey, A., et al. (1991). Cognitive-behavioral treatment of chronically parasuicidal borderline patients. *Archives of General Psychiatry, 48,* 1060–1064.

Linehan, M., Heard, H., & Armstrong, H., (1993). Naturalistic follow-up of a behavioral treatment for chronically parasuicidal borderline patients. *Archives of General Psychiatry, 50,* 971–974.

Lipsey, J., Robinson, R., Pearlson, G., et al. (1984). Nortriptyline treatment for post-stroke depression: A double-blind trial. *Lancet, 1,* 297–300.

Lipsey, J., Spencer, W., Robins, P., et al. (1986). Phenomenological comparison of post-stroke depression and functional depression. *American Journal of Psychiatry, 143,* 527–529.

Lipsius, S. (1991). Combined individual and group psychotherapy: Guidelines at the interface. *International Journal of Group Psychotherapy, 41,* 313–327.

Ludwig, A. (1987). The role of psychiatrists in the practice of psychotherapy. *American Journal of Psychotherapy, 41,* 361–368.

Mace, N., & Rabins, P. (1991). *The 36-hour day.* Baltimore: Johns Hopkins Press.

Mann, J. (1986). How medication compliance affects outcomes. *Psychiatric Annals, 16,* 537–570.

Manning, D., & Frances, A. (1990). Afterword. In D. Manning & A. Frances (Eds.), *Combined pharmacotherapy and psychotherapy for depression.* Washington, DC: American Psychiatric Press, 183–186.

Marder, S., Johnson-Cronk, K., Wirshing, W., & Eckman, T. (1991). Schizophrenia and behavioral skill training. In B. Beitman & G. Klerman (Eds.), *Integrating pharmacotherapy and psychotherapy.* Washington, DC: American Psychiatric Press, 311–328.

Marlatt, G., & Gordon, J. (Eds.), (1985). *Relapse prevention: Maintenance strategies in the treatment of addictive behaviors.* New York: Guilford.

Marman, C., Gaston, L., Gallagher, D., et al. (1989). Alliance and outcome in late-life depression. *Journal of Nervous and Mental Diseases, 177,* 464–472.

Masnik, R., Oloste, S., & Rosen, A. (1980). Coffee group: A nine year follow up study. *American Journal of Psychiatry, 137,* 91–93.

Mason, S., & Siris, S. (1992). Dual diagnosis: The case for care management. *American Journal on Addictions, 1,* 77–82.

Mattick, R., & Andrews, F. (1994). Social phobia. In M. Hersen & R. Ammerman (Eds.), *Handbook of prescriptive treatment for adults.* New York: Plenum, 157–178.

Mavissakalian, M. (1991). Agoraphobia. In B. Beitman & G. Klerman (Eds.), *Integrating pharmacotherapy and psychotherapy*. Washington, DC: American Psychiatric Press, 165–182.
Mavissakalian, M. (1993). Combined behavioral and pharmacological treatment of anxiety disorders. In J. Oldham, M. Riba, & A. Tasman (Eds.), *American psychiatric press review of psychiatry, Volume 12*. Washington, DC: American Psychiatric Press, 541–564.
Mavissakalian, J., Jones, B., Olson, C., et al. (1990). Clomipramine in obsessive-compulsive disorder: Clinical response and plasma levels. *Journal of Clinical Psychopharmacology, 10*, 264–268.
McConnaughy, E., DiClemente, C., Prochaska, J., et al. (1989). Stages of change in psychotherapy: A follow-up report. *Psychoth rapy, 26*, 494–503.
McKay, J. R., McLellan, A. T., & Alterman, A. I. (1992). An evaluation of the Cleveland criteria for inpatient treatment of substance abuse. *American Journal of Psychiatry, 149*, 1212–1218.
McNutt, E., Severson, S., & Schomer, J. (1987). Dilemmas of interdisciplinary outpatient care: An approach toward their amelioration. *Journal of Psychiatric Education, 11*, 59–65.
Medenwald, J., Greist, J., & Jefferson, J. (1990). *Carbomezapine and Manic Depression: A guide.* Madison, WI: Dean Foundation.
Mehlum, L., Fris, S., Iron, T., et al. (1991). Personality disorders 2–5 years after treatment: A perspective follow-up study. *Acta Psychiatrica Scandinavica, 84*, 72–77.
Millon, T. (1981). *Disorders of personality: DSM-III, Axis II.* New York: Wiley.
Moffic, S. (1982). A preliminary report in effects of initiating medication groups at a mental health clinic. *Hospital and Community Psychiatry, 33*, 387.
Munich, R. L., & Gabbard, G. O. (1992). Hospital psychiatry. In A. Tasman & A. Riba (Eds.), *Review of psychiatry, Volume 11*. Washington, DC: American Psychiatric Press, 501–502.
Munoz, R. (1994). Editorial: Commodity markets and the carving of psychiatry. *Clinical Psychiatry Quarterly, 17* (1) 1.
Murphy, G. E., Simons, A. D., Wetzel, R. D., et al. (1984). Cognitive therapy and pharmacotherapy, singly and together in the treatment of depression. *Archives of General Psychiatry, 41*, 33–41.
NIH Consensus Conference. (1992). Diagnosis and treatment of depression in late life. *Journal of the American Medical Association, 268*, 1018–1024.
Ost, L. (1989). One session treatment for specific phobias. *Behavioral Research and Therapy, 27*, 1–7.
Ostow, D. (1962). *Drugs in psychoanalysis and psychotherapy.* New York: Basic Books.
Otto, M., Gould, R., & Pollack, M. (1994). Cognitive-behavioral treatment of panic disorder: Considerations for treatment of patients over the long term. *Psychiatric Annals, 24*, 307–315.
Pearlson, G., & Robins, P. (1988). The late-onset psychoses: Possible risk factors. In D. Jeste & S. Zisook (Eds.), *The psychiatric clinics of North America.* Philadelphia: W. B. Sanders, 15–32.
Pollack, M., & Otto, M. (1994). Long-term pharmacologies treatment of panic disorder. *Psychiatric Annals, 24*, 291–298.
Porter, K. (1993). Combined individual and group psychotherapy. In H. Kaplan & B. Sadock (Eds.), *Comprehensive group psychotherapy (3rd ed.).* Baltimore: Williams & Wilkins, 314–324.
Post, F. (1962). *The significance of affective symptoms in old age.* (Maudsley Monograph No. 10). London: Oxford University Press.
Post, F. (1966). *Persistent persecutory states of the elderly.* Oxford: Pergamon.

Post, R. (1992). Transduction of psychosocial distress into the neurology of recurrent affective disorders. *American Journal of Psychiatry, 149,* 999–1010.

Post, R., Rubinow, D., & Ballenger, J. (1986). Conditioning and sensitization in the longitudinal course of affective illness. *British Journal of Psychiatry, 149,* 191–201.

Prezioso, F. A. (1994). Preserving inpatient care. *Behavioral Health Management, 14*(2), 22–29.

Pristach, C., & Smith, C. (1990). Medication compliance and substance abuse among schizophrenic patients. *Hospital and Community Psychiatry, 41,* 1345–1348.

Prochaska, J., & DiClemente, C. (1984). *The transtheoretical approach.* Homewood, IL: Dorsey Press.

Prochaska, J., & DiClemente, C. (1986). The transtheoretical approach. In J. Norcross (Ed.), *Handbook of eclectic psychotherapy.* New York: Brunner/Mazel.

Putnam, F. W. (1989). *Diagnosis and treatment of multiple personality disorder.* New York: Guilford.

Quitkin, F., Steward, J., McGrath, P., et al. (1993a). Loss of drug effect during continuation therapy. *American Journal of Psychiatry, 150,* 562–565.

Quitkin, F., Steward, J., McGrath, P., et al. (1993b). Further evidence that a placebo response to antidepressants can be identified. *American Journal of Psychiatry, 150,* 566–570.

Reding, M., Orto, L., & Winter, S. (1986). Antidepressant therapy after stroke: A double-blind trial. *Archives of Neurology, 43,* 763–765.

Rehm, L., LePage, J., & Bailey, S. (1984). Unipolar depression. In H. Hersen & R. Ammerman (Eds.), *Handbook of prescriptive treatment for adults.* New York: Plenum, 95–118.

Reid, W. (1989). *The treatment of psychiatric disorders: Revised for the DSM-III-R.* New York: Brunner/Mazel.

Robinson, R., Kubas, K., Starr, L., et al. (1984). Mood disorders in stroke patients: Importance of lesion location. *Brain, 107,* 81–93.

Rodenhauser, P., & Stone, W. (1993). Combining psychopharmacology and group psychotherapy: Problems and advantages. *International Journal of Group Psychotherapy, 43,* 11–28.

Rosenbaum, J., & Pollack, R. (1994). The psychopharmacology of social phobia and comorbid disorders. *Bulletin of the Menninger Clinic, 58*(suppl), 67–83.

Rosenheck, R., & Astrachan, B. (1990). Regional variation in patterns of inpatient psychiatric care. *American Journal of Psychiatry, 147,* 1180–1183.

Rounsaville, B., Klerman, G., & Weissman, M. (1981). Do psychotherapy and pharmacotherapy of depression conflict? *Archives of General Psychiatry, 38,* 24–29.

Rozanski, A., Bairey, C., Keantz, D., et al. (1988). Mental stress and the induction of silent myocardial ischemia in patients with coronary artery disease. *New England Journal of Medicine, 318,* 1005–1012.

Rush, A. (1988). Cognitive approaches to adherence. In A. Frances & R. Hales (Eds.), *The American psychiatric press review of psychiatry, Volume 7.* Washington, DC: American Psychiatric Press.

Rush, D., & Hollon, S. (1991). Depression. In B. Beitman & G. Klerman (Eds.), *Integrating pharmacotherapy and psychotherapy.* Washington, DC: American Psychiatric Press, 121–142.

Sabin, J. (1991). Clinical skills for the 1990's: Six lessons from HMO practice. *Hospital and Community Psychiatry, 42,* 605–608.

Sabin, J., & Borus, J. (1992). Mental health teaching and research in managed care. In J. Feldman & R. Fitzpatrick (Eds.), *Managed mental health care: Administrative and clinical issues.* Washington, DC: American Psychiatric Press.

Sabshin, M. (1987). The future role of psychiatrists. In C. Adelson & C. Rabinowitz (Eds.), *Training psychiatrists for the 90's. Issues and recommendations.* Washington, DC: American Psychiatric Press.

Sachs, G., Lafer, B., Truman, C., Noeth, M., & Thibaut, A. (1994). Lithium monotherapy: Miracle, myth and misunderstanding. *Psychiatric Annals, 24,* 299–306.

Sackett, D., & Haynes, R. (1976). *Compliance with therapeutic regimens.* Baltimore: Johns Hopkins University Press.

Salkovskis, P., & Kirk, J. (1989). Obsessional disorders. In K. Hawton, P. Salkovskis, J. Kirk & D. Clark (Eds.), *Cognitive behavior therapy for psychiatric patients: A practical guide.* Oxford: Oxford University Press, 129–168.

Salvendy, J., & Toffe, R. (1991). Antidepressants in group psychotherapy. *International Journal of Group Psychotherapy, 41,* 465–480.

Salzman, L. (1980). *Treatment of obsessive personality.* New York: Jason Aronson.

Salzman, L. (1989). Compulsive personality disorder. In T. Karasu (Ed.), *Treatments of psychiatric disorders.* Washington, DC: American Psychiatric Press, 2771–2782.

Sanders, F., & Feldman, L. (1993). Integrating individual, marital, and family therapy. In J. Oldham, M. Riba, & A. Tasman (Eds.), *American psychiatric press review of psychiatry, Volume 12.* Washington, DC: American Psychiatric Press, 611–629.

Santrock, J., Minnet, A., & Campbell, B. (1994). *The authoritative guide to self-help books.* New York: Guilford.

Sarti, P., & Cournos, F. (1990). Medication and psychotherapy in the treatment of chronic schizophrenia. *Psychiatric Clinics of North America, 13,* 215–228.

Schleifer, S., Macari-Hinson, M., Coyle, D., et al. (1989). The nature and course of depression following myocardial infarction. *Archives of Internal Medicine, 149,* 1785–1789.

Schneider-Braus, K. (1992). Managing a mental health department in staff model HMP. In J. Feldman, & R. Fitzpatrick (Eds.), *Managed mental health care.* Washington, DC: American Psychiatric Press, 125–141.

Schooler, N. (1994a). Engaging families in treatment effects outcomes. *Syllabus and proceeding summary American Psychiatric Association annual meeting.* Washington, DC: American Psychiatric Association, 64.

Schooler, N. (1994b). Maintenance treatment: Drug and psychosocial effects. *Syllabus and proceeding summary American Psychiatric Association annual meeting.* Washington, DC: American Psychiatric Association, 303.

Schou, M. (1991). Relapse prevention in manic depressive illness: Important and unimportant factors. *Canadian Journal of Psychiatry, 36,* 502–506.

Schroeder, N., & Keith, S. (1990). Role of medications in psychosocial treatment. In M. Herz, S. Keith, & J. Docherty (Eds.), *Handbook of schizophrenia, Volume 4.* New York: Elsevier, 45–67.

Sederer, L. I. (1992). Brief hospitalization. In A. Tasman & A. Riba (Eds.), *Review of psychiatry, Volume 11.* Washington, DC: American Psychiatric Press, 518–534.

Shakir, S., Volkmar, F., & Bacon, S. (1979). Group psychotherapy as an adjunct to lithium maintenance. *American Journal of Psychiatry, 136,* 455–456.

Shapiro, A., & Morris, L. (1978). The placebo effect in medicated psychological therapies. In S. Garfield & A. Begin (Eds.), *Handbook of psychotherapy and behavioral change: An empirical analysis, 2nd ed.* New York: John Wiley, 369–410.

Shapiro, D. (1965). *Neurotic styles.* New York: Basic Books.

Sharfstein, S. S. (1992). Managed mental health care. In A. Tasman & A. Riba (Eds.), *Review of psychiatry, Volume 11.* Washington, DC: American Psychiatric Press, 570–584.

Shear, M. (1991). Panic disorder. In B. Beitman & G. Klerman (Eds.), *Integrating pharmacotherapy and psychotherapy.* Washington, DC: American Psychiatric Press, 143–164.

Shock, N. (1984). In N. Shock (Ed.), *Normal human aging: The Baltimore longitudinal study of aging.* Washington, DC: U.S. Government Printing Office.

Siegler, J., Axelband, M., & Isikoff, J. (1993). Psychiatry: Taking a leadership role in managed health care. *Psychiatric Times.*

Siever, L. (1993). The frontiers of psychopharmacology. *Psychology Today, 27*(1), 40–44, 70–72.

Siever, L., & Davis, K. (1991). A psychobiological perspective on the personality disorders. *American Journal of Psychiatry, 148,* 1647–1658.

Soloff, P. H., Anselm, G., Nathan, R. S., et al. (1989). Amitriptyline vs. haloperidol in borderlines: Final outcomes and predictors of response. *Journal of Clinical Psychopharmacology, 9,* 238–246.

Sotsky, S., Galss, D., Shea, M., et al. (1991). Patient predictors of response to psychotherapy and pharmacotherapy: Findings in the NIMH treatment of depression collaborative research program. *American Journal of Psychiatry, 148,* 997–1008.

Sovner, R. (1991). A psychopharmacology service model. In C. Austad & W. Berman (Eds.), *Psychotherapy in managed care.* Washington, DC: American Psychological Association, 86–97.

Sperry, L. (1985). Treatment noncompliance and cooperation: Implications for psychotherapeutic, medical and lifestyle change approaches. *Individual Psychology, 41,* 228–236.

Sperry, L. (1995). *Handbook of diagnosis and treatment of the DSM-IV personality disorders.* New York: Brunner/Mazel.

Sperry, L., Gudeman, J., Blackwell, B., & Faulkner, L. (1992). *Psychiatric case formulation.* Washington, DC: American Psychiatric Press.

Spiro, H. (1986). *Doctors, patients and placebos.* New Haven, CT: Yale University Press.

Starkstein, S., Robinson, R., Berthrer, M., et al. (1988). Differential mood changes following basal ganglia vs thalamic lesions. Archives of Neurology, *45,* 725–730.

Steenbarger, B. (1994). Duration and outcome in psychotherapy: An integrative review. *Professional psychology: Research and practice, 25,* 11–119.

Stone, M. (1993). *Abnormalities of personality: Within and beyond the realm of treatment.* New York: Norton.

Stone, W., Rodenhauser, P., & Markert, R. (1991). Combining group psychotherapy and pharmacotherapy: A survey. *International Journal of Group Psychotherapy, 41,* 449–464.

Stoudemire, A., Fogel, B., Gulley, L., et al. (1993). Psychopharmacology in the medical patient. In A. Stoudemire & B. Fogel (Eds.), *Psychiatric care of the medical patient.* New York: Oxford University Press, 155–206.

Stoudemire, A., Hill, C., Morris, R., Martino-Saltzman, D., & Lewison, B. (1993). Long-term affective and cognitive outcome in depressed older adults. *American Journal of Psychiatry, 150,* 896–900.

Sullivan, M., Verhulst, J., Russo, J., & Roy-Byrne, P. (1993). Psychotherapy vs. pharmacotherapy: Are psychiatrists polarized? - A survey of academic and clinical faculty. *American Journal of Psychotherapy, 47,* 411–423.

Sussman, N. (1993). Integrating psychopharmacology and group psychotherapy. In H. Kaplan & B. Sadock (Eds.), *Comprehensive group psychotherapy, 3rd ed.* Baltimore: Williams & Wilkins, 363–371.

Swenson, C. R., & Wood, M. J. (1990). Issues involved in combining drugs with psychotherapy for the borderline patient. *Psychiatric Clinics of North America, 13*(2), 297–306.

Thompson, L., Florsheim, M., Gallagher, D., et al., (1986). Cognitive therapy with older adults. *Clinical Gerontologist, 5,* 245–270.
Thompson, L., Gallagher, D., & Breckenridge, J. (1987). Comparative effectiveness of psychotherapies for depressed elders. *Journal of Consulting and Clinical Psychology, 55,* 385–390.
Torrey, E. F. (1983). *Surviving schizophrenia: A family manual.* New York: Harper & Row.
Turner, R. (1992). Dynamic-cognitive behavior therapy. In T. Giles (Ed.), *Handbook of effective psychotherapy.* New York: Plenum, 437–454.
Uhde, T., & Tancer, M. (1991). Social phobia. In B. Beitman & G. Klerman (Eds.), *Integrating pharmacotherapy and psychotherapy.* Washington, DC: American Psychiatric Press, 435–446.
Vestal, R., Norris, A., Tobin, J., et al. (1975). Antipyrine metabolism in man: Influence of age, alcohol, caffeine, and smoking. *Clinical Pharmacological Therapy, 18,* 425–434.
Vestal, R., Wood, A., & Shaud, D. (1979). Reduced beta-adrenoreceptor sensitivity in the elderly. *Clinical Pharmacological Therapy, 26,* 181–186.
Vinagradov, S., & Yalom, I. (1989). *Concise guide to group psychotherapy.* Washington, DC: American Press.
Walrond-Skinner, S. (1986). *Dictionary of psychotherapy.* London: Routledge & Kegan Paul.
Ward, N. (1991). Psychosocial approaches to pharmacotherapy. In B. Beitman & G. Klerman (Eds.), *Integrating pharmacotherapy and psychotherapy.* Washington, DC: American Psychiatric Press, 69–104.
Warner, M. D., Griffin, M., & Peabody, C. (1993). High initial nortriptyline doses in the treatment of depression. *Journal of Clinical Psychiatry, 54,* 67–70.
Weissman, M., & Klerman, G. (1991). Interpersonal psychotherapy for depression. In B. Beitman & G. Klerman (Eds.), *Integrating pharmacotherapy and psychotherapy.* Washington, DC: American Psychiatric Press, 379–394.
Wells, K. B., Rogers, W. H., Davis, L. M., et al. (1993). Quality of care for hospitalized depressed elderly patients before and after implementation of the Medicare prospective payment system. *American Journal of Psychiatry, 150,* 1799–1805.
Wells, M., Glickhouf-Houghes, C., & Buzzel, U. (1990). Treating obsessive-compulsive personalities in psychoanalytic/interpersonal group therapy. *Psychotherapy, 27,* 366–379.
Westermeyer, J. (1991). Problems with managed care without a psychiatrist-manager. *Hospital and Community Psychiatry, 42,* 1221–1224.
Wilson, L., Lawson, I., & Brass, W. (1962). Multiple disorders in the elderly: A clinical and statistical study. *Lancet, 2,* 841–843.
Wilson, P. (1992). Relapse prevention: Conceptual and methodological issues. In P. Wilson (Ed.), *Principles and practice of relapse prevention.* New York: Guilford.
Winer, J., & Pollock, G. (1989). Psychoanalysis and dynamic psychotherapy. In T. Karasu (Ed.), *Treatment of psychiatric disorders.* Washington, DC: American Psychiatric Press, 2639–2648.
Wolf, P., Dauber, T., Thomas, H., et al. (1977). Epidemiology of stroke. In R. Thompson & J. Green (Eds.), *Advances in neurology, Volume 16.* New York: Raven Press, 5–19.
Wolpe, J. (1982). *The practice of behavior therapy, 3rd ed.* New York: Pergamon Press.
Woodward, B., Duckworth, K., & Guthiel, T. (1993). The pharmacotherapist-psychotherapist collaboration. In J. Oldham, M. Riba & A. Tasman (Eds.), *American psychiatric press review of psychiatry, Volume 12.* Washington, DC: American Psychiatric Press, 631–649.
Wyatt, R. (1994). *Practical psychiatric practice: Forms and protocols for clinical use.* Washington, DC: American Psychiatric Press.

Wynne, L. (1983). A phase-oriented approach to treatment with schizophrenics and their families. In W. MacFarlane (Ed.), *Family therapy in schizophrenia.* New York: Guilford Press, 251–265.

Yager, J., Anderson, A., Devlin, M., et al. (1993). Practice guidelines of eating disorders. *American Journal of Psychiatry, 150,* 212–228.

Yalom, I. (1985). *The theory and practice of group psychotherapy, 3rd ed.* New York: Basic Books.

Yesavage, J., Brink, T., Rose, T., Adey, M. (1983). The geriatric depression rating scale: Comparison with other self-report and psychiatric rating scales. In T. Crook, S. Ferris, & R. Bartus (Eds.), *Assessment in Geriatric Psychopharmacology.* CT: Mark Powley Associates, 154–165.

Young, J., Zonana, H., & Shepler, L. (1986). Medication noncompliance in schizophrenia: Codification and update. *Bulletin of the American Academy of Psychiatry and Law, 14,* 105–122.

Zaslav, M., & Kalb, R. (1989). Medicine as metaphor and medicine in group psychotherapy with psychiatric patients. *International Journal of Group Psychotherapy, 39,* 457–467.

Zitrin, C., Klein, D., & Woerner, M. (1978). Behavior therapy, supportive therapy, imipramine and phobias. *Archives of General Psychiatry, 35,* 307–316.

Zoler, M. (1994). Lithium-resistant bipolar patients benefit from combined treatment. *Clinical Psychiatry News, 11,* June.

Name Index

Alden, L., 134
Alterman, A. I., 152
American Psychiatric
  Association, 23, 151, 152
Ammerman, R., 74
Anderson, C., 119
Andrews, F., 92
Applebaum, P., 23, 26, 29
Appleby, L., 149
Armstrong, H., 37, 124
Astrachan, B., 141
Awad, G., 117
Axelband, M., 4

Baer, L., 135
Bailey, S., 108
Baird, M., 21, 50
Ballenger, J., 95, 103
Barlow, D., 83, 87, 134
Beaudry, P., 90
Beavers, R., 43
Beck, A., 108, 125
Beitman, B., 8, 16, 20, 21, 22,
  25, 26, 50, 54, 71, 79, 80
Benjamin, L., 134
Bennett, M., 11
Beutler, L., 13, 76
Bills, L. J., 151
Bisbee, C., 60, 61, 83, 101,
  110, 119
Blackwell, B., 7, 12, 20, 25, 26,
  49, 53, 54
Blair, K., 20
Bleuler, E., 168
Blotcky, M., 31
Blumenthal, J., 169
Borus, J., 7, 26
Brass, W., 156
Breier, A., 121
Brock, D., 63
Brook, D., 65, 87, 107, 110
Brotman, A. W., 151
Brown, R., 61
Budman, S., 5
Burns, D., 61
Busch, F., 21, 24, 25
Butler, G., 82, 84

Caine, E., 163, 168
Carlson, J., 59
Carney, R., 170
Chiles, J., 26
Chiverton, P., 168
Christensen, L., 63
Clark, D., 93
Clarkin, J., 9, 13, 22, 37, 40,
  43, 76, 83, 87, 98, 116, 130
Clement, S., 9
Coccaro, F., 129
Cochran, S., 100
Cournos, F., 117
Cowley, D., 81, 82
Craske, M., 86
Cummings, M. A., 148

Davenport, Y., 63, 98
Davis, J., 120
Davis, K., 125, 129, 132, 135,
  137
Dekle, D., 63
Deltito, J., 134
De Risi, W., 67
Diamond, R., 64
DiClemente, C., 14, 50
Docherty, J., 20, 49, 50, 51,
  55
Doherty, W., 55, 56
Duckworth, K., 25, 26, 131

Eastwood, M., 168
Eaton, W., 169
Eckman, T., 20, 63, 119
Elkin, I., 21, 35, 69, 105
Eryavec, G., 168
Fallon, I., 113
Faulkner, L., 12
Fava, M., 36, 69, 74, 111
Feldman, J., 5
Feldman, L., 45, 46
Field, M. J., 141
Fitzpatrick, R., 5
Fogel, B., 170
Frances, A., 9, 37, 40, 106,
  107, 130
Frank, E., 108
Friedmann, C., 64
Frolkis, V., 161
Fuerst, M., 96, 98, 101

Gabbard, G. O., 141, 143
Gelernter, C., 91
Giles, T., 4, 5
Glick, I., 22, 43, 83, 87, 98,
  108, 116, 119, 130
Goldberg, R., 167
Goldsmith, S., 22, 43, 83, 87,
  98, 116, 130
Goldstein, M., 57, 120, 121,
  122
Gonnella, J. S., 142
Goodwin, F., 97, 98, 99, 100,
  102, 146
Gordon, J., 68, 69, 73
Gould, E., 21, 24, 25
Gould, R., 85
Gray, B. H., 141
Greenblatt, D., 161
Greist, J., 37, 61, 82, 83, 85,
  86, 87, 88, 89
Griffin, M., 146
Grof, P., 147
Group for the Advancement
  of Psychiatry, 35
Grunes, J., 158
Gudeman, J., 12
Gunderson, J., 126

Guscott, R., 147
Guthiel, T., 25, 26, 29, 131

Hampson, R., 43
Haynes, R., 49, 55
Heard, H., 37, 124
Heimberg, R., 91
Heinz, J., 157
Herrmann, N., 168
Hersen, M., 74
Hinrichsen, G., 163
Hoberman, H., 109
Hogarty, G., 120, 122
Hollon, S., 37, 106, 111
Hooley, J., 111
Hyland, J., 8

Isikoff, J., 4

Jamison, K., 95, 96, 97, 99, 100, 102
Jaques, E., 9
Jefferson, J., 37, 61, 83, 85, 86, 87
Jenike, M., 87, 88, 135, 161
Joyce, P., 106

Kahn, D., 97, 100, 102, 148
Kaji, J., 36, 69, 74, 111
Kalb, R., 42
Kanas, N., 98, 115
Karasu, T., 35, 39
Katz, P., 8
Kavanaugh, D., 69
Kavoussi, R., 129
Kay, J., 26
Keck, P. E., 148
Keilholz, P., 163
Kelly, K., 25
Kennedy, J., 17
Kirk, J., 76
Kisch, J., 6
Klein, D., 83
Klerman, G., 8, 21, 28, 35, 68, 69, 106
Koenigsberg, H., 130, 131
Kraepelin, E., 165, 168
Kreisler, K., 151

Lansky, J., 168
Lawson, I., 156
LePage, J., 108
Lesser, I., 64
Leszcz, M., 158
Leuchter, A., 165
Lewis, J., 31, 59
Lewisohn, P., 61, 109
Liberman, P. B., 142
Liberman, R., 20, 62, 63, 65, 66, 67, 113
Liebowitz, M., 91, 134
Linehan, M., 16, 17, 37, 124
Lipsey, J., 168
Lipsius, S., 47, 48
Little, M., 64
Low, A., 120
Ludwig, A., 5, 8

Mace, N., 168, 169
Mann, J., 108
Manning, D., 106, 107
Marder, S., 118, 119
Markert, R., 39, 42
Marlatt, G., 68, 69, 73
Marman, C., 158
Masnik, R., 63
Mason, S., 118
Mattick, R., 92
Mavissakalian, M., 79, 80, 81, 82, 85, 87, 89, 90, 93
McConnaughy, E., 16, 50
McKay, J. R., 152
McLellan, A. T., 152
McNutt, E., 7
Mehlum, L., 136
Meuser, K., 67
Millon, T., 127
Moffic, S., 63
Mooney, J., 79, 80
Morris, L., 55
Munich, R. L., 141
Munoz, R., 9

National Institute of Mental Health, 35
NIH Consensus Conference, 162

Orto, L., 168
Ost, L., 93
Ostrow, D., 35
Otto, M., 84, 85, 86

Peabody, C., 146
Pearlson, G., 165
Perry, S., 9, 37, 40, 130
Phipps, C., 20
Pollack, M., 84, 85, 86
Pollack, R., 92
Pollock, G., 36, 126
Porter, K., 46, 47
Post, F., 165, 168
Post, R., 95, 103, 105
Prezioso, F. A., 143
Prochaska, J., 14, 50
Putnam, F. W., 150

Quitkin, F., 55, 69, 71, 72

Rabins, P., 168, 169
Reding, M., 168
Rehm, L., 108
Reid, W., 134
Robins, P., 165
Robinson, R., 168
Rodenhauser, P., 39, 40, 41, 42
Rosenbaum, J., 92
Rosenheck, R., 141
Rounsaville, B., 35
Roy-Byrne, P., 81, 82
Rozanski, A., 169
Rubinow, D., 95, 103
Rush, A., 108
Rush, D., 37, 106, 111

Sabin, J., 7, 26
Sabshin, M., 7
Sachs, G., 95
Sackett, D., 49, 55
Salkovskis, P., 76
Salvendy, J., 107
Salzman, L., 135
Sanders, F., 45, 46
Santrock, J., 61
Sarti, P., 117
Schleifer, S., 170
Schmidt, G., 7, 25, 26
Schneider-Braus, K., 3
Schomer, J., 7
Schooler, N., 121, 122
Schou, M., 96, 102
Sederer, L. I., 143
Sellers, E., 161
Severson, S., 7
Shader, R., 161
Shakir, S., 63, 65

Shapiro, A., 55, 127
Sharfstein, S. S., 142
Shaud, D., 161
Shear, M., 85
Shepler, L., 117
Shock, N., 160
Siegler, J., 4
Siever, L., 125, 129, 132, 135, 137
Siris, S., 118
Sotsky, S., 14
Sovner, R., 6
Spar, J., 165
Sperry, L., 12, 36, 49, 59, 80, 127
Spiro, H., 21
Stam, M., 134
Starkstein, S., 168
Steenbarger, B., 50
Stone, M., 37, 124, 126, 131, 135
Stone, W., 39, 40, 41, 42
Stoudemire, A., 163, 170
Strauss, J., 121
Sussman, N., 30, 42
Swenson, C. R., 153

Tancer, M., 91
Teasdale, J., 111
Thompson, L., 158
Toffe, R., 107
Torrey, E. F., 114
Turner, R., 128

Uhde, T., 91

Vestal, R., 160, 161
Vinagradov, S., 64, 116

Waddell, D., 83, 87, 134
Waikar, S, 86
Walrond-Skinner, S., 54
Ward, N., 20, 21, 50, 51, 52, 54, 55, 56, 57
Warner, M. D., 146
Weekes, C., 61
Weissman, M., 35, 106
Wells, K. B., 142
Wollo, M., 135
Westermeyer, J., 4
Wilson, L., 156
Wilson, P., 70, 73, 74, 126
Winer, J., 36, 126
Winter, S., 168
Woerner, M., 83
Wolf, P., 167
Wolpe, J., 79, 81
Wood, A., 161
Wood, M. J., 153
Woodward, B., 25, 26, 28, 29, 131
Wyatt, R., 60
Wynne, L., 116

Yalom, I., 64, 65, 116
Young, J., 117

Zaslav, M., 42
Zitrin, C., 83
Zoler, M., 98, 99
Zonana, H., 117

Subject Index

Action, psychiatrist evaluator role, 16
Aged. *See* Geriatrics
Agoraphobia
  combined treatment modalities, 37
  psychopharmacology for, 84–87
Alcohol abuse, schizophrenia, 117–118
Anorexia nervosa, inpatient treatment, 151–152
Anxiety disorders, 79–94
  generalized anxiety disorder, 90–91
  geriatrics, 166–167
  obsessive compulsive disorder, 87–90
  overview of, 79–80
  panic and/or agoraphobia, 84–87
  phobias
    simple phobias, 92–93
    social phobias, 91–92
  psychoeducation, 94
  treatment strategies, generally, 80–84
Anxious cluster personality disorders. *See* Personality disorders
Assessment
  anxiety disorders, 80–82
  relapse/recurrence prevention, 69–72
Audiotapes, relapse/recurrence prevention, 76
Avoidant personality disorder
  described, 133
  treatment guidelines, 133–134

Bibliotherapy. *See also* Psychoeducation
  anxiety disorders, 94
  bipolar disorder, 101, 103–104
  depression, 109–110, 112
  personality disorders, 137
  psychoeducation, 60–61
  schizophrenia, 122
Bipolar disorder, 95–104. *See also* Depression
  combination therapy for, 96–99
  inpatient treatment, 148–149
  medication adherence, 99–101
  overview of, 95
  psychoeducation, 101–102, 103–104
  relapse/recurrence prevention, 102–103
Booster sessions, relapse/recurrence prevention, 74
Borderline personality disorder
  combined treatment modalities, 37
  described, 127–128
  inpatient treatment, 153–154
  treatment guidelines, 129–131
Bulimia nervosa, inpatient treatment, 151–152

Cardiac disease, geriatrics, 169–171
Cerebrovascular disease, geriatrics, 167–169
Certification and licensure, nonmedical therapist, 6
Charting, inpatient treatment, 145–146
Cognitive-behavior therapy, combined treatment modalities, 37
Collaboration
  legal considerations in, 28–29
  pharmacotherapist-psychotherapist
    described, 24–25
    guidelines for, 26–28
  three-way, 26
Combined treatment modalities, 35–48
  family therapy and psychopharmacology, 43–44
  group therapy and psychopharmacology, 39–42
  individual psychotherapy and family therapy, 44–46
  individual psychotherapy and group therapy, 46–48
  individual psychotherapy and psychopharmacology, 38–39
  multiple combinations, 48
  overview of, 35–37
  prerequisite guidelines for, 38
  relapse/recurrence prevention, 74

Compliance. *See* Medication adherence
Confidentiality, legal considerations, 28
Consultor role, of psychiatrist, managed care, 23–31
Contemplation, psychiatrist evaluator role, 16
Countertransference
bipolar disorder, 99–100
borderline personality disorder, 130–131
group therapy, psychopharmacology and, 42

Demography, aged and, 157
Dependent personality disorder
described, 132
treatment guidelines, 134
Depression, 105–112. *See also* Bipolar disorder
cardiac disease, 171
combination therapy for, 105–108
combined treatment modalities, 36, 37
major
inpatient treatment, 146–148
older adults, 162–165
medication adherence, 108
obsessive compulsive disorder, 88
overview of, 105
psychoeducation, 109–110, 112
relapse/recurrence prevention, 111–112
stroke and, 168, 169
Desensitization, anxiety disorders, 79–80, 82
Diagnosis
DSM-IV categories, 11, 13
psychiatrist evaluator role, 11–19
Discharge guidelines, inpatient treatment, 144–145
Dissociative disorders, inpatient treatment, 150–151
Dramatic cluster personality disorders. *See* Personality disorders
DSM-IV
combined treatment modalities, family therapy and psychopharmacology, 43
diagnosis, 11, 13
personality disorders, 124, 126
Dynamic Cognitive Behavior Therapy (DCBT), dramatic cluster personality disorders, 128–129

Eating disorders, inpatient treatment, 151–152
Eccentric cluster personality disorders. *See* Personality disorders
Education. *See also* Psychoeducation
nonmedical therapist, 6
psychiatrist consultor role, 26
Elderly. *See* Geriatrics
Electroconvulsive therapy, older adults, 165, 169, 171
Evaluation guidelines, inpatient treatment, 142–143
Evaluation psychiatrist evaluator role, 11–19
Evaluator role, of psychiatrist, managed care and, 11–19
Explanatory model, medication adherence, 50–51

Family factors, medication adherence, 55–58
Family intervention strategies, schizophrenia, 116, 119, 121
Family therapy
bipolar disorder, 97–98
borderline personality disorder, 130
depression, 107–108
psychopharmacology and, combined treatment modalities, 43–44
psychotherapy and, combined treatment modalities, 44–46
Fee-for-service, managed care compared, 7

Generalized anxiety disorder, psychopharmacology for, 90–91
Geriatrics, 156–171
anxiety disorders, 166–167
cardiac disease, 169–171
overview of, 156–157
psychiatric disorders, 162–164
psychopharmacology, 160–162
psychosis, late onset (paraphrenias), 165–166
psychotherapeutic considerations, 157–158
stroke, 167–169
treatment guidelines, generally, 159–160
Global Assessment of Functioning (GAF) Scale, 17
Global Assessment of Relationship (GARF) Scale, 17
Group therapy. *See also* Medication groups
anxiety disorders, 87

Group therapy (*continued*)
bipolar disorder, 98
depression, 107
individual psychotherapy and, combined treatment modalities, 46–48
medication groups, psychoeducation, 62–65
psychopharmacology and, combined treatment modalities, 39–42
schizophrenia, 115–116

Hallucination, inpatient treatment, 147
Handouts. *See* Patient handouts
Heart disease, geriatrics, 169–171
Histrionic personality disorder, described, 127
Hospitalization. *See* Inpatient treatment

Identity. *See* Professional identity
Individual psychotherapy. *See* Psychotherapy
Informed consent, legal considerations, 28–29
Inpatient treatment, 141–155
bipolar disorders, 148–149
borderline personality disorder, 153–154
changes in, summary table, 155
charting, 145–146
depressive disorders, 146–148
discharge guidelines, 144–145
dissociative disorders, 150–151
eating disorders, 151–152
evaluation guidelines, 142–143
overview of, 141–142
schizophrenia, 149–150
schizotypal personality disorder, 136–137
substance abuse disorders, 152–153
treatment guidelines, 143–144
Irrationality, medication adherence, 50–51
Late onset psychosis (paraphrenias), geriatrics, 165–166
Leadership style, psychiatry and, 9
Legal considerations, collaboration and, 28–29
Licensure. *See* Certification and licensure
Long-term therapy, short-term therapy compared, 5–6

Maintenance, psychiatrist evaluator role, 16
Major depressive disorders
inpatient treatment, 146–148
older adults, 162–165
Malpractice, legal considerations, 29
Managed care, 3–31
psychiatrist consultor role, 23–31
psychiatrist evaluator role, 11–19
psychiatrist provider role, 20–22
role change and, 3–10
Managerial role, psychiatry and, 9
Medication adherence, 49–58
anxiety disorders, 82–83, 86–87
bipolar disorder, 99–101
borderline personality disorder, 130
depression, 108
family factors, 55–58
overview of, 49–50
patient factors, 50–55
personality disorders, 126
schizophrenia, 117–118
Medication groups
depression, 110
psychoeducation, 62–65
described, 62–63
treatment guidelines, 63–65
schizophrenia, 119
Millon Clinical Multiaxial Inventory (MCMI), medication adherence, 52–53

Narcissistic personality disorder, described, 127
Noncompliance. *See* Medication adherence

Obsessive compulsive disorder, psychopharmacology for, 87–90
Obsessive-compulsive personality disorder
described, 132–133
treatment guidelines, 135
Older adult. *See* Geriatrics
Outcomes
inpatient treatment, 141–142
managed care psychiatry, 7–8

Panic, psychopharmacology for, 84–87
Paraphrenias (late onset psychosis), geriatrics, 165–166
Patient education, psychoeducation, 60. *See also* Psychoeducation
Patient handouts, psychoeducation, 60–61. *See also* Psychoeducation
Pattern, psychiatrist evaluator role, 13
Perpetuants, psychiatrist evaluator role, 13
Personality disorders, 124–137
anxious cluster disorders, 131–135

avoidant personality disorder, 133
dependent personality disorder, 132
obsessive compulsive personality disorder, 132–133
overview of, 131–132
treatment guidelines, 133–135
borderline personality disorder, 129–131
combined treatment modalities, 37
dramatic cluster disorders, 126–129
borderline personality disorder, 127–128
histrionic personality disorder, 127
narcissistic personality disorder, 127
overview of, 126–127
treatment guidelines, 128–129
eccentric cluster disorders, 135–137
overview of, 135–136
schizotypal personality disorder, 136
treatment guidelines, 136–137
medication adherence, 126
overview of, 124
psychoeducation, 137
relapse/recurrence prevention, 126
treatment strategies, generally, 124–126
Personality style
medication adherence, 51–53
relapse/recurrence prevention, 72–73
Phobia
agoraphobia, combined treatment modalities, 37
simple phobias, psychopharmacology for, 92–93
social phobias, psychopharmacology for, 91–92
Placebo effect, medication adherence, 54–55
Precontemplation, psychiatrist evaluator role, 14
Presentation, psychiatrist evaluator role, 13
Professional identity
professional role contrasted, 3–4
proposed changes in, 6–10
Professional role
evaluator role, psychiatrist, 11–19
professional identity contrasted, 3–4
proposed changes in, 6–10
Projective identification, psychiatrist consultor role, 24–25
Provider role, of psychiatrist, 20–22
Psychiatric nursing, role change in, 5–6
Psychiatry
consultor role, managed care, 23–31
evaluator role, managed care and, 11–19
proposed role for, 6–10
provider role, managed care, 20–22
role change in, 3–4
Psychoeducation, 59–67. *See also* Education
anxiety disorders, 83, 94
bipolar disorder, 101–102, 103–104
depression, 109–110, 112
medication groups, 62–65
described, 62–63
treatment guidelines, 63–65
overview of, 59
personality disorders, 137
schizophrenia, 118–120, 122–123
symptom management training, 65–67
types of, 59–62
patient education, 60
patient handouts and bibliography, 60–61
self-help organizations and support groups, 61–62
Psychology, role change in, 5–6
Psychopharmacology
combined treatment modalities, 35–48
family therapy, 43–44
multiple combinations, 48
overview of, 35–37
prerequisite guideline for, 38
consultor role, 24–28
family therapy and, combined treatment modalities, 43–44
geriatrics, 160–162
group therapy and, combined treatment modalities, 39–42
outcomes and, 8
psychiatrist provider role, 20–22
psychiatry and, 9–10
psychotherapy and, combined treatment modalities, 38–39
Psychosis
inpatient treatment, 147
late onset (paraphrenias), geriatrics, 165–166
Psychosurgery, obsessive compulsive disorder, 89

Psychotherapy
  family therapy and, combined treatment modalities, 44–46
  group therapy and, combined treatment modalities, 46–48
  psychiatrist consultor role, psychopharmacology, 24–28
  psychiatry and, 8–9
  psychopharmacology and, combined treatment modalities, 38–39
  schizophrenia, 114–115

Quality, psychiatry and, 9

Readiness, medication adherence, 50
Regimen modification, medication adherence, 53–54
Relapse/recurrence prevention, 68–76
  anxiety disorders, 83–84
    generalized anxiety disorder, 91
    obsessive compulsive disorder, 89–90
    panic and/or agoraphobia, 87
    social phobias, 92
  biopsychosocial components, 68–69
  bipolar disorder, 102–103
  depression, 111–112
  guidelines, 69–76
    assessment, 69–72
    integration with treatment, 73–74, 76
    personality style, 72–73
  overview of, 68
  personality disorders, 126
  schizophrenia, 120–122
  worksheet for, 75
Ritual, obsessive compulsive disorder, 88–89
Role. *See* Professional role
Role change, managed care and, 3–10

Schizophrenia, 113–123
  combined treatment for, 114–116
  inpatient treatment, 149–150
  medication adherence, 117–118
  overview of, 113–114
  psychoeducation, 118–120, 122–123
  relapse/recurrence prevention, 120–122
Schizotypal personality disorder
  described, 136
  treatment guidelines, 136–137
Self-help groups. *See also* Psychoeducation
  anxiety disorders, 94
  psychoeducation, 61–62
Short-term therapy, long-term therapy compared, 5–6
Simple phobias, psychopharmacology for, 92–93
Social phobias, psychopharmacology for, 91–92
Social work, role change in, 5–6
Splitting
  borderline personality disorder, 131
  combined treatment modalities
    group therapy and psychopharmacology, 42
    individual psychotherapy and group therapy, 46–48
  psychiatrist consultor role, 24–25
Stages of change, medication adherence, 50
Stroke, geriatrics, 167–169
Substance abuse, schizophrenia, 117–118
Substance abuse disorders, inpatient treatment, 152–153
Suicide
  dissociative disorders, 150
  inpatient treatment, 145, 146
Support groups. *See also* Psychoeducation
  anxiety disorders, 94
  bipolar disorder, 102, 104
  depression, 110, 112
  psychoeducation, 61–62
  schizophrenia, 120, 123
Surgery. *See* Psychosurgery
Symptom management training, psychoeducation, 65–67

Tailoring, combined treatment modalities, 36
Therapeutic relationship, medication adherence, 54–55
Three-way collaboration, 26
Transference, borderline personality disorder, 130–131
Treatability, psychiatrist evaluator role, 14
Treatment capability, psychiatrist evaluator role, 16–17
Treatment expectation, psychiatrist evaluator role, 14
Treatment modalities, combined. *See* Combined treatment modalities
Treatment willingness, psychiatrist evaluator role, 14